Christian Liberty Nature Reader

Book Four

Revised and Edited by
Edward J. Shewan

Christian Liberty Press
Arlington Heights, Illinois

General editorship by Michael J. McHugh
Revised and edited by Edward J. Shewan
Copyediting by Belit Shewan and Diane Olson
Cover design by Eric D. Bristley
Layout and graphics by Edward J. Shewan
Graphics by Christopher D. Kou

A publication of
Christian Liberty Press

502 West Euclid Avenue
Arlington Heights, IL 60004
www.christianlibertypress.com

ISBN 978-1-930092-54-9
        1-930092-54-7

Set in Berkeley
Printed in the United States of America

TABLE OF CONTENTS

Preface

We are honored to bring you a classic textbook. This particular textbook is designed to not only improve a student's reading skills and comprehension, but to also increase the student's understanding of and interest in God's wonderful creation.

To be able to read is to have the foundation for all subsequent education. The child whose reading training is deficient grows up to become the child who is frustrated, in despair, and soon to join the ranks of the drop-outs, the pushed-outs, the unemployed and the unemployable.

Millions of Americans are handicapped in their reading skills. The "look-say" method of teaching, rather than the older "phonics" technique, has resulted in a generation of functional illiterates. It has been revealed that the U.S. literacy rate has dropped to the level of Burma and Albania and is rapidly approaching that of Zambia.

Not only is the method of teaching reading of vital importance, but also the literary quality of the reading material. So much of what passes for "modern" readers in education today is nothing more than pablum that stresses "social adjustment."

The Bible says we are to do "all for the glory of God" (I Corinthians 10:31). Reading for God's glory necessitates reading material that draws attention to

Him and His truth, that reflects His majesty, and that meets the standards of the Holy Scriptures. What this means is that we should take any reading selection to Philippians 4:8 and ask these simple questions: "Is it true? Is it noble? Is it right? Is it pure? Is it lovely? Is it admirable? Is it excellent? Is it praiseworthy?"

As we look at the American readers of days gone by we find that the Biblical standard was followed. Such readers featured the finest British and American authors who emphasized God, morality, the wonders of creation, and respect for one's country.

The *Christian Liberty Nature Reader Series* follows the pattern of the past. Believing that the student can gain an enhanced appreciation for God by studying His creation (Psalm 19:1; Romans 1:20), this textbook seeks to present the majestic splendor of His handiwork.

It is our prayer that this series will give to the reader the joy that is to be associated with "good reading," and that the knowledge imparted will help "make wise the simple" (Psalm 19:7).

Dr. Paul D. Lindstrom

Chapter One
Perching Birds

The Quail

Did you ever take a walk in the country and suddenly hear a **whirring**, or buzzing, sound? Do you remember how you stood still, too frightened to move, and then you saw a few brown birds sailing away? The noise you heard was made by some quails as they flew up quickly from the ground. They saw you first and lost no time in taking wing.

The quail is about as big as a **bantam** chicken. Its color is brownish like that of dried-up grass; its body is short and plump; and its bill is short and stout like that of a chicken. Its short, round wings help it to fly up quickly from the ground and then it sails away, usually in a curved flight. The quail's wings always make a loud, whirring sound when it begins to fly, and this is what usually frightens people when they are walking along. By the time they recover from their fright, the quails are some distance away, for they can fly very fast.

The quail has short, stout legs like the chicken; and, on each foot, it has three toes toward the front and a short one toward the back. This back toe is like a heel and helps the bird to walk. Its claws are short and strong; with them, it can scratch for bugs.

The quail's nest is on the ground among tall grasses and weeds, and is so cleverly hidden that one could pass by it a hundred times and not see it. The mother quail scratches a little **hollow**, or hole, in the ground and lines it with grass. She will lay as many as fifteen white eggs. They are round at one end and very pointed at the other; and her eggs are smaller than a hen's eggs.

The mother quail is so cautious that she never goes straight to her nest. First she enters a patch of weeds some distance from the nest and then quietly sneaks along until she reaches it. Her color is so much like that of the grass and leaves about her that one cannot see her on the nest at all. God created her with brownish feathers to protect her from foxes, coyotes, and hawks; her protective color is called **camouflage**.

As soon as the cute baby quails hatch, they are able to run about in the grass. They look like little, fluffy chicks with downy **plumage**; they also have brown, striped backs. The mother quail trains her babies just as a mother hen trains her brood of chicks. She teaches them how to scratch for bugs and how to hide and keep quiet when she gives the alarm. Later, when the danger has past, she clucks to call them together again.

The father quail also helps take care of the babies. His call is a clear whistle, "Bob White! Bob White!" but his mate's call sounds like, "Will you come? Will you come?" If you learn to imitate his mate's call, he will answer you and even come to your hiding place.

If you are kind to the quails, the whole family may visit your garden to eat bugs, and they will enjoy taking dust baths there, too. Some of them may even have their singing lessons there. How you will laugh to hear them! The father quail himself calls loud and clear, "Bob White! Bob White!" Then the little male quails try to call just as he did. He calls again and they try again, for they seem to have a hard time learning to whistle just right, but they do not get tired and quit. They keep on trying and trying.

Some quails were once heard having their singing lesson in a vegetable garden. The little "Bob" could be heard quite plainly. That did not seem so very hard to whistle, but such a time they had

trying to whistle the "White!" They called, "Bob! Bob!" several times; then they whistled "Bob Wh! Bob Wh!"; and finally a sharp "Bob White!" Don't you think they were proud and happy to get it exactly right?

Quails eat a great many insects that harm the farmers' crops and also a great many weed seeds. If these seeds were allowed to grow, they would crowd out the little plants in the fields. The quails are really the farmers' friends.

Quails do not fly south when winter comes but remain with us throughout the year. In the fall, they go about in flocks called **coveys** (kŭv´•ēs), and we can help them by putting out food where they can find it when the ground is covered with ice and snow.

Review

1. How can you recognize a quail when you see one?

2. How do quails resemble chickens?

3. How do they escape an enemy?

4. Why can we say that the quails are the farmers' friends?

5. How can we help quails?

Some Things To Do

Watch quails during the fall and put out food for them in winter. Learn to imitate the quails' calls and see if you can **coax**, or gently persuade, them to come to you. Listen for their singing lessons in early summer.

The Brown Thrasher

Listen to that beautiful song! It reminds one of the mockingbird, but it is the song of a brown thrasher. The brown thrasher is reddish-brown, while the mockingbird is gray. The thrasher is a little larger than a robin; and its back, wings, and tail are the color of cinnamon. Its white breast is streaked with brown, its eyes are yellow, and its bill is slightly curved. A thrasher is usually seen in bushes or thickets. Its long tail is the bird's "**rudder**" and helps it to dodge in and out among the twigs.

The brown thrasher makes its nest in a bush, vine, or **brush** pile. It makes a large foundation of twigs, which are laid crisscross, in and out, and are interwoven in a wonderful way. No person, aided by his two hands, could make it more firm, if he tried. It looks so much like the branches and twigs near it that many people never discover it.

The "mattress" is composed of bits of leaves and soft rootlets.

A pair of thrashers were nesting in a rose vine and both birds looked so much alike that one could not tell the male from the female. They worked on the "mattress" from six until nine o'clock for three mornings. One scratched and pecked at the soil near a bush until it found a piece of an old leaf that just suited it. Picking it up, the bird looked around to make sure nobody saw it, and then flew to its **nesting site**—the place where it was building its nest. It did not fly straight to its nest but entered the vine a little distance from it, and sneaked along through the branches. It did not want anyone to know its secret.

Later, there were five brown, speckled eggs in the nest. The mother bird allowed

her friends to approach very near while she was **brooding**—that is, while she was sitting on the eggs to hatch them; she carefully turned the eggs with her bill as a hen does when brooding. When it rained, she fluffed out her feathers over the edge of the nest so that the raindrops ran off her feathers and splashed outside the nest.

When the baby thrashers hatched, they were naked and helpless, and their mouths seemed so very large. Every time a branch near the nest was gently touched, up went the little heads with mouths wide open, for the baby birds were always hungry. One day the father bird brought a big grasshopper which he tried to feed to them, but it was too large for the little birds to swallow. He flew down to the concrete walk and beat the grasshopper until it seemed that he would break his bill. When he had beaten it almost to a **pulp**, he returned to the nest and succeeded in feeding it to one hungry baby. Even then the little fellow had quite a mouthful; and, after gulping it down, he blinked his eyes and settled down in the nest. He had had enough for a while. Each baby was fed in its turn, and altogether they ate hundreds of bugs and grew fast. Soon they were ready to leave the nest.

One afternoon the thrashers were heard calling out on the lawn; the mother bird was giving a young one flying lessons. The little fellow was so timid that he was afraid to hop or try his wings. The mother bird came with a **wireworm** in her bill and flew down about three feet from him. Though he was so hungry that he begged and begged for it, she remained where she was and coaxed him to come. But she had to coax a while before he took courage to hop toward her. As he hopped, he had to open his wings to balance himself. When he reached her, she fed him the wireworm and then chirped to him. Don't you think that she must have praised and encouraged him? He remained there in the grass, blinking his bright eyes, while she flew away to get another bug. He opened and closed his wings, too, and this helped to strengthen them.

When the mother returned, she had a big, plump grasshopper, and she stayed about seven feet away from the young thrasher. She coaxed and coaxed until he hopped over to her, using his wings to balance himself, and then she fed it to him and chirped to him again. While she flew away to get another bug, he remained where he was, opening and closing his wings and blinking his eyes.

When his mother returned, he did not see her for she perched on the lowest branch of a bush about five feet away. This branch was about five inches from the ground. She called until he discovered where she was, and then how she had to coax him to come! He hopped over there but was afraid to hop up on the twig. Such a time they had! One would think she would loose her patience with him, but no! She just kept coaxing and coaxing. Finally, he hopped up beside her and she fed him. How good that worm must have tasted, for he had worked so hard for it! He remained there on the twig while she flew away again.

There was a plum tree in the poultry yard, and in the late afternoon the little thrasher was discovered perching on a branch about six feet from the ground, as quiet as a mouse. This tree was about a hundred feet away from the bush where he learned to hop up on a branch. Do you not think that he did well to reach the tree?

Thrashers eat thousands of insects, many of which would harm plants. They are friendly birds and like to nest in yards and gardens. They also like to perch high in a tree when they sing.

Once a man won the confidence of a thrasher that nested in his garden and every afternoon it perched in a tree near him to sing. He whistled a few notes softly while the bird cocked its head and listened. He whistled the tune several times and then the thrasher tried to imitate him.

If one learns to recognize the thrasher's alarm call, he may be able to help. Whenever the bird discovers a cat, snake, owl, or other enemy, it utters its alarm call. You can help it then by chasing its enemy away.

Late one afternoon, the thrasher's alarm was heard near a road. Investigation proved the cause of the disturbance to be an owl sitting on a branch in a sycamore tree about five feet away from the thrasher's nest. Both birds were making a dreadful fuss about it. The owl was driven from the tree, but it was some time before the birds became quiet again.

God made the North American brown thrasher to **migrate**. This means it flies south in the fall and returns north in the spring.

Review

1. What is the difference between a brown thrasher and a mockingbird?

2. How does the thrasher's long tail help it?

3. Why do few persons see thrashers' nests?

4. How do the young birds learn to fly?

5. Of what use are brown thrashers?

Some Things To Do

Watch a thrasher flying through bushes to see how it uses its tail as a rudder. Watch one singing in a tree to discover how it balances itself on the twig. Try to get a brown thrasher to answer your call.

The Cardinal

Here is one of the most interesting and attractive birds that God has created. The male has bright-red feathers and a thick, red bill. The color of his bill and feathers and the size of his bill give him the name cardinal (deep, rich red) grosbeak (large beak). Notice his beautiful topknot, or **crest**. He can raise and lower it. The cardinal grosbeak is about as big as a robin but more plump, and is bright red all over except for his black throat. His

mate is not red but a beautiful pinkish-brown with a pink bill.

Early one morning, a male cardinal visited a yard and inspected all the bushes and vines. Two days later, he brought his mate to show her the places that he liked. Although he called and called her, she was very independent and pretended that she did not hear him. She would not come until he flew back to get her. He seemed to say something to her to coax her from bush to bush and vine to vine, but none of the places suited her. She had her own ideas about where to build. Soon they flew away again, in search of a better place. When the cardinal's mate finds a place that she likes, he helps her with the work.

A pair of cardinals once built their nest in a cedar tree. They used bark, rootlets, and grasses. The male caught hold of the bark on a wild grape vine with his bill, held tight, and pulled on it as he **hovered** in the air—flapping his wings and fluttering in one place. He carried this long strip of fine bark to his mate, who was working on the nest. They both seemed quite happy over this particular piece, and he was so proud because he had pleased her that he began to sing. They lined the nest with fine rootlets and grasses to make a nice, soft "mattress." Four pretty, reddish-brown eggs with white spots were laid in the nest.

At first the cardinal was very attentive to his mate, even feeding her seeds. Later, when she was brooding, he sometimes forgot about her and she had to call and call him. One afternoon she even had to go out after him and make him come home to help her.

Another pair of cardinals were found in a garden. He was hopping among the young plants, peering this way and that. Finally, he pecked a bug from one plant and ate it; then he found another and quickly hopped over to the grape **arbor**, calling loudly. Suddenly his mate flew down from the farther end of the arbor, and he fed her the bug he had found.

The cardinal sings a pretty song that sounds like, "What cheer! What cheer!" As he sings, his crest begins to rise, and when he is in the middle of his song, it stands up straight. He perches on a branch near the top of a tree when he sings, usually on an outer branch where everybody can see and hear him. He is so proud and bold! Do you not think that his mate is anxious about him then? Some enemy might see his bright red color and hear his song.

Cardinals eat bugs, seeds, and wild berries, being especially fond of grapes and cedar berries. It seems that wherever many cedar trees are found in the woods, cardinals are sure to be seen.

When the ground is covered with snow, the cardinals cannot find much food. If you will feed them, they will come to your yard every day for crumbs and grain. You must not let a cat come into your yard if you feed the birds, for even a good cat will catch a bird when you are not watching. Cats are natural enemies of birds.

Review

1. How can you recognize a cardinal when you see one?

2. How do cardinals make their nests?

3. How can you help them in winter?

Some Things To Do

Feed cardinals grain and **suet**, or animal fat, during cold weather. Watch a cardinal sing. Notice how he balances himself while singing, and watch his crest rise and fall.

The Purple Martin

Did you ever watch a beautiful purple bird flying gracefully through the air? It climbs high on tireless wings, then coasts downward, dodges in and out, up and down. If it happens to fly near a pond, lake, or river, it takes a drink as it flies. This is the purple martin, North America's largest swallow.

The purple martin is smaller than a robin and its feathers are bluish-black and very glossy; but the female and the young birds are brownish with gray breasts. Its bill is short and opens very wide. Its strong wings are long and narrow, and the tail

is somewhat forked. Its legs and feet are not very strong, but it can perch. Each of its feet has three toes toward the front and one toward the back.

It is an expert flier, catching all of its food while on the wing. Its tail is like a rudder, helping it to dodge and turn quickly when flying. It eats nothing but bugs, and since it is so very active, it must eat thousands of them. It eats many mosquitoes and harmful beetles that destroy plants, and will attack a hawk or crow and chase it away.

If you build a birdhouse that has more than one room, purple martins may rent them. Some people put out **gourds** on a pole, with an entrance hole cut in each gourd. Purple martins like to live in birdhouses near people and near each other;

they are **sociable** birds and nest in groups. They keep up a cheerful twittering and **warble** short, sweet songs.

Sparrow

Put your birdhouse up early and try to prevent the sparrows from nesting in it. Often when the martins arrive from the south, they find the sparrows in their house and then there is a lively battle. Sometimes the sparrows are compelled to leave, but frequently they use one or two rooms while the martins take the others. Then one martin is always on duty guarding the entrances to their rooms, and one sparrow watches the doors to the sparrow apartments.

The martins' white eggs are laid on a "mattress" of fine straw, grass, and feathers. The young birds eat so many insects that they grow very rapidly, and then they have their flying lessons and learn how to catch bugs while flying.

One day in August, a **colony**, or group, of purple martins were holding a tournament. All were assembled on the roof and porches of a two-story, twelve-room birdhouse. Several adult birds bowed and twittered to each other beautifully as though they were discussing something important, but the others were quietly listening. Then one moved over to a young bird and bowed and twittered to it. Immediately, the young one took wing, circled, climbed high in the air, coasted down, turned, dodged this way and that, and then landed gracefully on the porch. You should have heard the twittering then! They seemed to be proud of the young bird's skill. Each one was given a chance to show how well it could fly, and upon its return, there was much twittering and bowing. This continued all afternoon. Then, with much warbling and twittering, all flew away and did not return until the following spring. God in His wisdom designed purple martins to migrate in the fall so they can find plenty of food during winter.

If a purple martin sees a cat, it gives its alarm call and dives down until it seems that it will perch on the cat's back. It checks its flight when very near its enemy and climbs upward again, only to repeat the performance. This annoys the cat so much that it often jumps up and strikes at the bird with its paw. When the bird is just quick enough to escape the cat's blow each time, the cat finally gives up and runs away.

Since purple martins eat so many harmful bugs, they are one of the most helpful birds known to man; we should attract them to our yards by erecting colony birdhouses.

Review

1. Describe the purple martin.

2. Why is it such an expert flier?

3. Why do we say it is a sociable bird?

4. Of what use is it?

5. How can we attract purple martins?

Some Things To Do

Erect a colony birdhouse for purple martins early in spring. Observe how gracefully they fly, how they catch insects, and how they get a drink while flying.

The Kingbird

Have you ever seen some small birds attacking a crow or hawk and chasing it? They were kingbirds, but some people call them "bee-martins" because they like to raid **apiaries**—places in which colonies of bees are kept. North American kingbirds are a little smaller than robins. The Eastern kingbird's head, back, wings, and tail are a dark bluish-gray; its underparts are white; and there is a white band across the bottom of its tail. The Western kingbird has light gray plumage and yellow underparts, with whitish edges on the tip of its tail feathers. On the crown

of both of these North American kingbirds is a hidden red crest which can be seen only when it raises the feathers on its head.

God gave the kingbird a strong bill that has a slight hook and opens very wide. At its base are some bristles that help it when it catches insects. Its strong wings help it to fly fast, and its tail is an excellent rudder to help it turn. Its legs are strong; and it has feet with three toes that point toward the front and one that points toward the back, allowing it to perch.

It perches on a wire, fence, or tree. When its sharp eyes spy an insect, it darts out after it, snaps it up, and returns to its perch to watch for another one. It is one of our flycatchers. Watch a kingbird catch an insect; see how quickly it darts out from its perch, and how sharply it turns in the air after catching an insect. You can even hear its **mandibles**, the upper and lower parts of its bill, click as it snaps up the bug.

The kingbird builds high in a tree and uses rootlets and grasses to make a firm, neat nest. The eggs are light with brown spots. The baby birds are always hungry and are fed hundreds of insects. The kingbird does much good because it eats many harmful beetles and other insects. It also eats **robber flies** which destroy our honey bees. Though it eats bees, too, the bees it eats are mostly **drones**. Whenever it spies a crow or hawk, it attacks and drives it out of the neighborhood.

Even though the kingbird does not sing and its call is harsh, we should protect it because it is so brave and so helpful to man. It flies to Central or South America for the winter but returns to North America in the spring.

Review

1. How can you recognize a kingbird when you see one?

2. Why is it called a flycatcher?

3. Of what use is it to man?

Some Things To Do

Watch a kingbird pursuing a crow or hawk. Can you tell why the crow or hawk does not turn and try to attack the kingbird?

The Crow

"Caw! Caw! Caw!" Just listen to those crows! Did you ever hear birds make such a racket? The crow is larger than a pigeon, has glossy black feathers, and is quite pretty in the sunlight. Its bill is thick, pointed, and very strong. The crow can use it to dig a hole, to carry a fish or a little chicken, to catch big grasshoppers, and to tear bark from vines. It even fights with its bill.

The crow constantly flaps its large, strong wings when flying. Since its flight seems slow and

29 23 29

clumsy, we say that it is **lumbering** through the air. Its legs are very strong and the long toes have strong claws. Three toes point toward the front and one toward the back. Its long back toe helps it to perch in a tree. It can walk as well as hop; and, as it walks along, it is always busy looking for food. It eats almost anything, alive or dead.

The crow's large nest is high up in a tree and is made of sticks, twigs, grasses, and bark from vines, with a "mattress" of grass and soft bark. In the nest are four, bluish-green eggs with brown spots. When the babies hatch, they are not covered with **down**, like little chickens and turkeys, but are naked and helpless like the baby robins and bluebirds. The adult crows catch many insects for them and also steal baby birds and little chickens to feed them. We are sorry that they do this, because they do so much good the rest of the year. They eat hundreds of grasshoppers, beetles, caterpillars, and other insects, and they even eat mice.

Crows like corn, too. When the farmer's corn is sprouting, they pull it up and have a feast. While the flock of crows is feeding in the field, a few of them act as **sentinels**, or guards, and are perched high up in trees. When some have eaten, they exchange places with the sentinels, so that all may get food. Every crow in the flock takes its turn on guard duty. If the sentinels see a man or boy with a gun, they caw loudly; and then away they all fly after their sentinels. Often they  will not fly if the person does not have a gun, for they seem to know whether he has a gun or not.

Sometimes a farmer puts a scarecrow in his field. He puts old clothes on big sticks out in the middle of the field, and hopes to frighten the crows away by making them believe it is a man. They do stay away for a while, but later they all fly down and eat more than ever. If, instead, the farmer coats his seed corn with coal tar, they are not so likely to pull it up when it is sprouting, and the corn will not be injured.

Crows do not migrate. In winter, hundreds of them gather in a forest. Every morning they fly far away to get food, and every evening they return. We say that such a forest is a "crows' roost." In spring, they separate again, flying in all directions;

NATURE READER BOOK 4

and the next winter, when housekeeping cares are over, they again are found at the roost.

Crows help one another. They always work together and seem to obey orders, too. They are very wise. A young crow makes an interesting pet and will follow its owner everywhere. It is sure to get into mischief and may even get others into trouble because of its pranks.

Review

1. What is the difference between a crow and a pigeon?
2. How does a crow fly?
3. What do crows eat?
4. How do they help one another?
5. What is a crows' roost?

Some Things To Do

Watch crows in a field to see how they work together. Notice how alert the sentinels are, and how much confidence the whole flock has in them.

Chapter Two
Birds of Prey

The Owl

Did you ever spend a night in the country where you heard voices that sounded like some person laughing? "Whoo, whoo, whoo, whwhoo, to-whoo-ah!" repeated several times in deep tones—the last two descending the scale. When uttered by several large barred or hoot owls, these voices are enough to frighten any person, though owls probably like to hear it.

There are about fourteen different kinds of owls in the United States and Canada, and most of them are **nocturnal**; that is, they sleep during the day and do their hunting at night. They differ in size, but all have very soft, fluffy feathers which make them look larger than they really are. The owls' feathers are tipped with down, making their flight absolutely noiseless, so that rodents have no warning of their dreaded enemy's approach. If one is studying birds in the woods early in the morning he may be surprised to see a large barred owl flying silently about four feet above his head.

All owls look wise, with their flat faces and large, round eyes set deep in the front of their heads, so that they see a creature with both eyes at once. Other birds have their eyes in the sides of their heads. Our eyes are in the front of our heads, too, but we can roll them to see on either side of us. Owls cannot do this, but must turn their heads to look sideways. If anyone walks around an owl, it will turn its head to follow him with its eyes; and when it is looking almost straight behind itself, it turns its head back to the front and around to the other side so quickly that it looks as though it turned its head all the way around.

Owls seem to have no necks; their heads appear to be set directly on their shoulders.

An owl's eyes are large and round, reminding one of a cat's eyes; but when it contracts its eyes, the **pupils** are round, while those of a cat are narrow and long, like slits. At night the pupil in an owl's eye is expanded until it covers most of the eye, for its sight is very keen at night, although it can see but little during the day. The stiff feathers around an owl's eyes do not lie flat like those of other birds; they **radiate**—or spread outward in all directions—from around each eye and probably help the owl to focus its sight.

Other birds, such as thrashers, are afraid of owls and often get greatly excited over the presence of one in the same tree. They sometimes make a dreadful fuss about it, while the owl merely turns its head and looks at them.

The owl's short, strong, sharp beak is almost hidden by the feathers on its face, and the upper part is hooked so that it can tear its prey. All birds that eat live animals and tear their prey have strong, sharp, hooked beaks. The two parts of a bird's bill or beak are called the upper and lower mandibles. When an owl is angry, it snaps its mandibles together, making a loud, frightful noise. A screech owl kept in a cage for a day snapped its mandibles angrily whenever some boys came near it. When the boys fed it ground meat, the owl just swallowed it; but when they put a large piece of meat into the cage, the owl held it down firmly with its feet, tore off bits of meat with its beak, and gulped them down. Though it was watched closely, nobody saw the owl take a drink. Evidently its food both quenches its thirst and satisfies its hunger.

Owls have large, strong wings that help them carry their prey while flying; and their tails serve as rudders to guide their flight. Their legs are very strong and are covered completely to the claws with feathers that are nearly as fine as hair. On each foot, there are four strong toes tipped with powerful, curved, sharp, needle-pointed claws, called **talons**; they are as strong as a steel trap. Three toes point toward the front, and one points toward the back. Owls can move their outer toes forward or backward, as you can move your thumbs, to get a firm grip on its victim.

The owl has a very keen sense of hearing, and follows the sound of an animal as it moves along. When it gets close, the owl extends its talons, strikes the back of the victim's neck, sinks its talons into its prey, locks its toes, and flies away with it. If its prey is small, the owl may carry it in its beak.

Owls eat every bit of their
victims—bones, feathers, fur,
and all. Later, they vomit
little balls or **pellets**,
consisting of the
indigestible parts
of the meal. If one
looks carefully,
he can see these
pellets on the
ground in the
woods or wherever

**Tawny
Owl**

owls perch. If one of these balls is examined,
what the owl ate can be easily determined. The
bits of hair, bone, or feathers can be plainly seen.
If a number of pellets are seen beneath a tree, it is
probable that an owl is resting on a branch near
the trunk of the tree. One must look closely,
however, because the owl's color is so much like
that of the tree's bark that it escapes notice.

Birds can lock their toes by bending their legs,
and then unlock them by straightening their legs.
Did you ever notice chickens roosting on the
perches in a henhouse? After **alighting**, or
landing, on the perch, the chicken squats down
on it, bending its legs. Then it tucks its head
beneath its wing and goes to sleep. It never falls
off the perch while asleep because its toes are

locked and cannot straighten themselves while the legs are bent. When the chicken awakes, it must stand up straight to unlock its toes; then it can fly down from the perch.

Owls do much good eating **rodents** and other animals that are pests to the farmer. They are especially fond of rabbits, gophers, squirrels, mice, and **weasels**. Sometimes they eat a bird or two, but not often. If the farmer's chickens roost in trees during the night, the great horned owl is likely to get one of them; but the chickens should be in the henhouse where they belong at night.

Some men were wrecking an old **silo** when they discovered a nest of four baby monkey-faced, or barn owls, in the top of it. One of them suggested dropping the **owlets** to kill them quickly, but another said that he would take them home and try to care for them until they could take care of themselves. He climbed up and down that silo four times to bring the babies down, for he could carry only one at a time. He took them six miles away to his home, forced them to swallow some finely ground meat, and put them into a cage outdoors.

The next morning, when he went out to see the new family, he was surprised to find four dead gophers laid in a row in front of the cage, and wondered how they had been brought there. He threw one of them into the cage to see what would happen. Immediately one of the owlets began to swallow it whole, head first, letting the tail hang out while it gradually gulped it down. Then the man threw the other three gophers into the cage, and the other owlets also had a good meal. Every morning for a week, there were four dead gophers beside the cage.

Then the man and his family decided to take turns watching during the night to see the owlets' visitor or visitors. They saw three adult owls bringing the gophers each night. Later, they began to bring more, sometimes seven, then nine;

and one morning there were twelve dead gophers beside the cage, and those owlets ate every one of them. It would be interesting to know how the adult birds located the little ones, for the man took them six miles away from the old silo where he found them.

When they were old enough to fly, the man left the cage door open. An adult owl perched in a tree nearby and coaxed the owlets until they flew up beside her. Then she flew to a telephone pole a short distance away and repeated the call, coaxing them to fly there. Finally they were able to fly quite well. Then they left their benefactor, but, frequently, one or two of them returned for a short time.

A man who was interested in owls and their food visited a pair of barn owls every night and kept a record of the food they brought to their nest for ninety-six nights. He found that they brought in 750 rats and mice, and only two birds. The largest catch in one night consisted of eighteen mice and nine rats.

Owls nest very early, often in January or February, and they use the same nest year after year. They usually select a cavity in a tree where their eggs will be safely hidden. These cavities may be the old homes of woodpeckers. Some owls nest in barns or old buildings, while others nest in old **burrows** of the ground squirrels and prairie dogs. Owls mate for life, but if one dies, the survivor will choose another mate.

Owl eggs are white, very round, and differ in size according to the **species**. The great horned owl's eggs are the size of the average egg of a hen; while those of the little screech owl, elf owl, and ground or burrowing owl are very small.

Owlets, like other baby birds, are always hungry and eat fully as much as their own weight in food every night. A half-grown barn owl was fed all the mice it would eat. It swallowed eight, one after another, and nearly ate the ninth one, letting the tail hang out of its mouth. However, it soon gulped that one down, too, and, in a few hours, ate four more mice. One man  collected and examined 675 pellets, and found that the owls had eaten 1,596 mice, 134 rats, 54 shrews, and 37 other animals. This menu tells us that owls are very valuable to the community where they nest and hunt, and they surely deserve protection from man.

During the winter, owls seldom migrate because they can get plenty of food. When rabbits are scarce in Canada, however, the beautiful large snowy owl comes southward into the northern part of the United States to hunt.

Yellow Owl

Since owls are more often heard than seen, **superstitious** people (those who have foolish fears of what is unknown or mysterious) believe that these birds have unusual powers and dread them. On the other hand, in ancient Greek **mythology** (made-up stories about pagan gods and goddesses), owls were sacred to Minerva, the pagan goddess of "wisdom." Due to this Greek fable, the owls' expression of thoughtfulness, and their silence, some people think of them as being wise. Others, however, think owls must know many things that are hidden from other creatures, since they can see in the dark. In addition, the ancient Romans looked upon owls with distrust and feared their presence, because they were considered messengers of death. God, however, simply created these creatures to live and eat; and, if they happen to hunt mice in somebody's yard, some foolish people hold superstitious ideas about them. Owls know nothing about such ungodly things, but the more mice they catch, the happier they are.

According to the Bible, all owls—both great and small—are considered unclean; this means that these birds of prey should not be eaten (Leviticus 11:17, Deuteronomy 14:16). God declared certain animals unclean to help His people understand what it meant to be holy; God also called His people to be holy as He is holy, and He still does so today (Leviticus 11:44, 45; Ephesians 1:4, 5:27; 1 Peter 1:15, 16). The Bible also states that owls are found in desolate regions throughout the Holy Land—inhabiting olive gardens, rocky areas, thickets, and ruins and tombs; they represent loneliness of heart (Job 30:29; Psalm 102:6) and the result of God's judgment (Isaiah 13:21, 34:13; Jeremiah 50:39; Micah 1:8). Therefore, the Bible rightly views God's creatures, the owls, and their habits, as opposed to the foolish ideas of man.

The Barn Owl

Barn owls, or monkey-faced owls, nest in hollow trees and deserted buildings, especially old towers. They are the most odd-looking of all the owls and do not have the wise expression of their relatives. They also do not have **tufts** of feathers around their ears; and their flat, heart-shaped faces remind people of monkey faces. Their plumage is beautiful—the light-colored feathers radiating from their eyes being **fringed**, or edged, with pretty brown feathers. Yellow, brown, and golden feathers blend beautifully on its head, back, wings, and tail. Its breast is light with many tiny dots of brown. All its feathers are extremely soft, fluffy, and silky—both in appearance and to the touch.

One day, a barn owl was observed sitting on the first egg it laid. About two weeks later, six owlets were found in the nest. The adult birds carried field mice in their beaks, grasping them by the back of the neck, to feed their young. The owlets ate them head first, swallowing as much as possible and letting the rest hang out of their beaks. Then they swallowed continually, until they gulped them down. In about seven weeks, the owlets were large and able to fly, though their parents still provided food for them. As they grew older, they no longer hissed

Barn Owl

when disturbed but became absolutely silent and motionless; in this way, they escaped notice.

Several owlets that had been banded, or tagged, were shot a few months later from one to four hundred miles away from the place where they were raised. This proves that they travel quite a distance from their old home. People, however, do not need to shoot owls because, even though they are unusual creatures and frighten us at times, they are really the world's best **mousers**. It has been estimated that one pair of field mice would probably multiply to one million in a year if all lived. We can readily see that these mice would become terrible pests were it not for God's mousers—the owls, hawks, and snakes. Therefore we should protect owls and speak a good word for them whenever we have the opportunity.

The Great Horned Owl

The great horned owl is the largest and most powerful of the common owls and lives in thickly wooded regions of North and South America. It is about twenty-two inches long, and its wingspan is nearly two and one-half feet long. Its color is brown and **tawny mottled**—marked with spots or blotches of dull, yellowish brown—so that one cannot see it easily as it rests on a branch near the trunk of a tree during the day. The two tufts of feathers on its head are about two inches long and resemble ears, but they are merely ornaments.

This owl uses the old nest of a crow, squirrel, or hawk that is high in a tree, or a large cavity in a tree. If one is a close observer, he can locate its nest by the brownish bits of downy feathers

Great Horned Owl

clinging to the branches, for when the owl enters and leaves the nest, the downy tips of its feathers are worn off by catching on the twigs. In February, the owl lays two or three—rarely more—round white eggs about the size of a hen's egg and begins to brood, or sit on them, as soon as the first egg is in the nest. When the owlets hatch, they are covered with a warm coat of fluffy down. Moreover, their heads and beaks are so very large compared to the size of their bodies that, for about two weeks, they must slide their beaks on the bottom of the nest when they move around. They are not yet able to lift their heads!

The adult birds keep a continual supply of food near their babies, so they can eat more than their own weight in food every night. This enables them to gain about an ounce a day for the first month. After that, most of their food is used in making feathers. When about five weeks old, they are fluffy and cute but mean in **disposition**, or attitude. They hiss and snap their mandibles when disturbed and spread their wings until they look very large. If the mother owl is as far as a quarter of a mile away, she will hear the alarm call of her owlets and hurry home to defend them.

The great horned owl spends the day hiding in trees, perching very close to the trunk, where its feathers blend so well with the bark that one can hardly see it. When a bird's color helps it to hide, we say it uses camouflage to protect it. The owl stretches itself to its full height, and its feathers lie close so that it looks very tall; but the owl can also fluff out its feathers and look twice its normal size.

The call of the great horned owl is similar to that of the barred owl; but it is uttered on the same tone, "Whoo-hoo-hoo! Whoo-hoo-hoo-hoo!"—like the deep, low-pitched sound of a dog barking in the distance. Sometimes this owl utters a piercing scream that makes one tremble. It is very courageous, daring, skillful, and helpful, destroying countless numbers of harmful rodents, such as gophers, rats, and rabbits. It may even get a chicken roosting in a tree during the night, but that is not the owl's fault, for the chicken should really be in the henhouse. The only time the great horned owl migrates is when food is hard to find.

The Barred Owl

Barred Owl

The barred owl—one of North America's largest owls—is darker in color than the great horned owl. It has "**bars**," or stripes, on its breast and has very dark eyes; but it does not have ear tufts on its very round head. It lives in the woods but is sometimes found near cities and in cemeteries. In March, it lays two to four round white eggs in a hollow tree or in the old home of a crow or hawk. When they hatch, the owlets of this bird of prey have a warm, fluffy coat of down and are fed many mice, gophers, and other small animals. They eat more than their own weight in food every night, so they grow very rapidly.

The barred owl's call, heard early in the evening and just before dawn, sounds almost human. If one learns to imitate it, he will be thrilled to find the owl answering and flying toward him. When half a mile away, one can hear its deep voice calling, "Whoo, whoo, whoo, wh-whoo, to-whoo-ah"; and then, perhaps, two or three will have a concert—

one **hooting** very rapidly, and another hooting in a higher tone, but all ending together on the "whoo-ah." One may be quite frightened until he realizes that the sounds are made by owls, and then he becomes interested and listens intently. Sometimes the owl will utter a terrible scream like a wild animal, and frighten all who hear it. If a crow sees an owl where it is resting against the trunk of a tree during the day, it will gather a large number of its friends together, and then the entire flock will worry the owl until it leaves.

Barred owls do not catch **poultry**—chickens, turkeys, ducks, and geese—and should be protected because they destroy so many rodents that are harmful.

The Screech Owl

The screech owl is common even in our city parks, where it can hide during the day because its color and shape resemble a knot on a tree. It is either brown-speckled or grayish, with two tufts of feathers on its head, which look like ears, but they are merely ornaments. The screech owl nests in old homes of woodpeckers, where it lays five little, rounded, white eggs. When they hatch, the owlets are helpless. They have warm coats of fluffy down, and their heads are large compared to the size of their bodies. They are fed many grasshoppers, crickets, beetles, caterpillars, field mice, small reptiles, spiders, **crayfish**, scorpions, earthworms, and sparrows; they also eat more than their own weight in food every night.

Screech Owl

The screech owl often stores enough food in a hollow tree to last about a week, so that it may be used when the weather is not favorable for hunting. During the day, the owl rests in a tree very close against the trunk, where it is quite safe because its color blends so well with that of the bark. At dusk, it stretches to its full height, **preens**—or smooths with the beak—its feathers, and stands on the alert for the least sound of a creature moving. Then the owl steals away on silent wings to seize its victim.

The screech owl's song is a **tremulous**, or quivering, whistle that is very unusual, descending the scale from a high-pitched tone, like a mournful cry. It does not migrate as some birds do. We should encourage the screech owl to live in the community, for it is valuable in helping to rid the neighborhood of mice and other pests.

The Saw-whet Owl

The saw-whet owl is brownish in color and smaller than a screech owl, but it has no ear tufts of feathers. Its little round white eggs are laid in the old nest of a woodpecker in a tree trunk. When the owlets hatch, they are covered with a warm coat of fluffy down, but are helpless. They are fed countless numbers of mice. In fact, the food of all saw-whet owls consists largely of mice. They do much good and should be protected.

During the day this little owl rests on a branch near the trunk of the tree, where its camouflage is so perfect that nobody notices it. If one happens to discover it, he can get very near and almost touch it before it will fly away. Its call is very **metallic**, like the sound made by a large-toothed saw when it is being **whetted**, or sharpened.

The Short-eared Owl

The short-eared owl is yellowish-brown with white spots above and pale in color below, with streaks on its breast; it also has very short ear tufts of feathers. It can be seen flying low over the grasslands early in the evening in search of meadow mice. This stocky bird of prey prefers the open country and is often seen traveling during the day.

Short-eared Owl

Frequently the short-eared owl lives in a colony—a group of owls, or other creatures, that live together. It lays four to seven round white eggs in a nest of grass on the ground. When the owlets hatch, they are covered with a warm coat of fluffy down and are fed countless numbers of mice, not to mention many small birds, insects, and frogs. This owl should be protected because it destroys so many mice.

The Long-eared Owl

The long-eared owl is brownish in color—mottled and barred—and has white underparts with dark streaks; and its ear tufts are very long. It lives in the forest and lays its round white eggs in the old nest of a crow or hawk. The long-eared owl usually

Long-eared Owl

raises a large brood—a number of babies hatched at one time—but not all live to become adults. Its food is largely mice and other rodents, birds, insects, snails, frogs, spiders, and crayfish. Its call is a scream. The long-eared owl should also be protected for it destroys many harmful creatures.

The Burrowing Owl

The burrowing owl is a remarkable little fellow that lives in the prairie lands of the Western Hemisphere, from southwestern Canada to the southern tip of South America. One can often see it during the day perching on a fence post along the road. It nests in the ground in the old burrow of a ground squirrel or prairie dog. The six little, round, white eggs are laid deep in the burrow in a nest of finely broken horse manure, which furnishes a soft "mattress" for them and keeps them warm even if the ground is damp. This owl eats many mice, grasshoppers, and crickets; but it drinks no water, probably because it gets enough moisture from its food. It is one of our most useful birds.

The Elf Owl

In the desert regions of Mexico and southwestern parts of the United States, we find the little elf owl that is about the size of a sparrow. Although it is the most common bird living in the cactus deserts, it may also inhabit forests, dry grasslands, and wet savannahs. The elf owl has a round head which is large compared to the rest of its body, and it has big yellow eyes. This smallest of the owls likes to make its home in the old nest of a woodpecker in a giant cactus that is as tall as a tree. It eats beetles, grasshoppers, moths, and little animals that it catches while flying at night.

The Snowy Owl

The large, handsome snowy owl is white with flecks of brown or dark-gray on its wings, back, and tail. Its face, throat, and breast are pure white. Its legs, feet, and talons are entirely covered by long, thick, white feathers, that look and feel like coarse hair. Its powerful beak is hidden by the stiff white feathers radiating from its eyes. Its large round eyes are yellow, and its head is very round but has no ear tufts of feathers.

This owl builds its nest on the ground, lining it with feathers. Its round, white eggs are the size of a large hen's egg. When they hatch, the owlets are covered with a warm coat of fluffy down.

The snowy owl is one of the few owls that is **diurnal**—that is, it flies about during the day

Snowy Owl

hunting for food. When resting in winter, it perches in a snow-covered tree, where one can hardly notice it because its coloring so closely resembles that of the bark and snow. It eats countless numbers of rats, mice, and other harmful rodents, which makes it a very useful bird. It lives in Canada, but migrates to the northern part of the United States when food is scarce there in winter.

Review

1. How can you recognize an owl when you see one?

2. How do owls differ from other birds?

3. What do owls eat?

4. How has God fitted them for getting their food?

5. How do they eat their prey?

6. Why do some call the owl a wise bird?

7. What does the Bible say about the owl?

8. Give an interesting fact about the barn owl, great horned owl, barred owl, screech owl, saw-whet owl, short-eared owl, long-eared owl, burrowing owl, elf owl, and snowy owl.

9. Why should owls be protected?

Some Things To Do

Listen to some owls and try to imitate their call. Notice if they call at the same time each evening. When you and one of your parents are in the woods, look for owl pellets. Examine these pellets to see what the owls ate; be sure to wear gloves to protect your hands from any diseases the owls may carry. Observe the trees carefully, to see if you can discover where the owls might be perching.

When you spot an owl, notice where and how it is resting, but do not frighten it. Observe how it follows you with its eyes as you walk around the tree. Notice if it returns to the same tree every day to rest. Try to hide near that tree at twilight to observe how the owl awakes and how it begins its day. Remember that one of your parents should be with you at all times, when doing this activity.

Chapter Three
Studying Birds

A Quiet Approach

Just think how much larger you are than a little bird! Is it any wonder that birds fly away when they see persons approaching them? If we really want to study birds, we should dress and act in such a way that they will not become frightened. We should wear clothes that are not brightly colored, and should not have fluttering or dangling ribbons or cords.

Walk quietly and slowly toward the birds you hear; and, when you see one, do not call to your friends or you will frighten it away. If you are not alone, all of you should agree upon a certain signal to use when one of you discovers a bird—perhaps raising a hand above your head, keeping it near your body as you raise it;

Spotted Flycatcher

for any sudden movement will startle a bird. Move cautiously and noiselessly, stopping often to look about you.

When you have approached near enough to study the birds' actions, stand perfectly still as though you were a part of the landscape. If you can do this, you will find that the birds will not pay any attention to you, and you will be rewarded by seeing them do many interesting things. Sometimes they act like feathered clowns.

Another good plan is to sit down near a little stream and be very quiet and patient. You will see birds coming to drink and bathe, and they will not notice you at all. If you practice kissing the back of your hand, or whistling, you will be able to imitate the calls of some birds, and you may even succeed in having them answer you.

One bird lover sat quietly and patiently in the woods near the place where a spring bubbled out of the ground and filled little hollows in the road. She kissed the back of her hand, making sounds similar to bird calls. According to the sounds produced, cardinals, thrushes, **towhees**, goldfinches, **indigo buntings**, wrens, and warblers approached very near, answering as they came. The beautiful goldfinches and indigo buntings even took their baths within a few feet of her. A white-throated sparrow nearly brushed her face with its wings as it flew past. Quietly, she approached a ruby-throated hummingbird and stood within four feet of it while it perched on a low wire, preened its feathers, and scratched its little head. It was just a mite of a bird but very particular about its appearance.

Goldfinches

Watching Hummingbirds

One day, a birdwatcher was sitting under a tree reading when she heard the hum of wings. Looking about, she saw a mother hummingbird teaching her two little ones how to get food from flowers. The mother approached a flower on a rose of Sharon bush, **probed**—or carefully examined—it with her bill, and then watched while the two young ones did the same thing. Then the three flew away but returned in a little while. The mother lagged behind and let the young ones approach the bush first. Would you believe that

they actually flew to two withered flowers and began to probe them? The mother uttered a little squeak and they flew to her side. Then she again showed them how to probe a fresh flower, and all three flew away. Later they returned a second time, and again the mother bird let the young ones approach the bush first.

Again those little birds tried to probe two withered flowers. She uttered a little squeak, and again they flew to her side. Once more she showed them which flowers to probe, and then they flew away. Within an hour the hum of their wings was heard again, and this time the young birds probed two fresh flowers.

Then the mother bird seemed to reward them, for they played a game of "cross tag," the way boys and girls play it. One little bird flew around, the other one flew after it, the mother bird flew between them, and the second little one then flew after the mother. Finally the mother bird darted into the middle of a honeysuckle vine on a trellis and perched on its stem. She uttered little squeaks while the two young ones flew around the bushes in the yard looking for her. Suddenly one discovered her hiding in the vine, and away they all flew. That was like the game of "hide-and-seek" that children play.

Hummingbirds frequently probe petunias and **salvia**, a type of mint plant, for food; and they perch on twigs near flowers to rest. If you learn to recognize the hum of their wings, you will be surprised at how often you can see hummingbirds.

Look For Color

An important thing to remember is to have the sun at your back when you look at a bird, for, otherwise, you will not see its true colors. If you look toward the light, a blue bird will appear black, and so will a brown bird. On a gray day, when it is cloudy or foggy you cannot see a bird's true colors for most of them will appear very dark.

It is a good plan to have a small notebook in which you may keep a record of the date, the time of day—whether it is morning, noon, afternoon, twilight, or night—and also the size of the bird—whether it is about as large as a sparrow, robin, pigeon, chicken, duck, or goose. Notice its general color, and the color of its back, breast, wings, and tail. Look carefully for any distinctive marks, such as a black cap; a line through the eye; marks on its breast, throat, back, wings, or tail; a crest, or topknot; and "bars," or stripes, in the wings or tail feathers.

Some birds have **flash colors** and these show only when the bird is active; that is, when it flies, opens its wings, or spreads its tail. Flash colors are usually white, but the cedar waxwing's are yellow. The flicker's flash color is on its rump or the lower part of its back. The flash colors of

Cedar Waxwing

the meadow lark, vesper sparrow, and blue-gray gnat catcher are on both sides of the tail. Some, like the kingbird, have the flash color across the bottom of the tail, and others have them in the corners of the tail, but many have no flash colors at all. We believe that the flash colors help birds to follow each other during migration.

Beaks, Wings, and Tails

If you can get near a bird, notice whether its beak is long or short, broad or narrow, thick or slender, straight or curved, pointed or hooked at the tip, and strong or weak. Looking at a bird's beak will help you determine the kind of food it eats. Woodpeckers have long, straight, pointed, strong beaks to chisel holes in the trees and get out the **grubs**. Birds with short, pointed, and stout beaks, like the sparrows, eat weed seeds. Their beaks have sharp edges to crack the seeds.

Creepers have slender beaks to probe the bark for insects and insect eggs. Ducks have broad, flat bills to hold the

Brown Creeper

food while the water is strained out at the sides of the bill. Birds of prey have very strong, hooked beaks for tearing flesh; while hummingbirds have long, slender beaks for reaching into the hearts of flowers to get **nectar** and tiny insects there.

If you see a bird fly, notice its wings. Some birds, like swallows and swifts, have very long, narrow, strong wings, for they feed "on the wing," capturing many insects. Birds with short, round wings, like the quail, can make a quick flight from an enemy but do not fly a long distance. Birds

Wing of a Hawk

with large wings, like hawks and eagles, usually soar or float in the air while scanning, or carefully examining, the ground for food.

Also notice how a bird holds its tail when it flies. When a blackbird flies, its tail looks like the keel of a boat; the mourning dove's tail is very pointed; and the barn swallow's tail is forked. Watch the bird as it flies, for some

Tail of a Barn Swallow

birds fly in a wavelike line, others fly in a jerky manner, and yet some fly in a straight line. Some flap their wings constantly, others flap them and then close them and dip, some flap their wings and then

Mallard

sail, and others fly as though it were hard work for them. Observe also the general shape of the bird as it flies, for each kind of bird has its own particular way of flying and looks different from any other bird. Even if the day is cloudy and you cannot see the colors of birds, you can identify them by their flight through the air or their actions on the ground.

Rescuing Birds

Notice whether a bird is quiet and slow, or restless and active, and whether it is bold or shy. Listen carefully to its call and song, so that you will be able to recognize it the next time you hear it. Notice whether it calls or sings while it flies—for some of our birds do, while others do not.

White-winged Crossbill

When an enemy is near, or if it is in distress, a bird utters a certain call and, if you learn to recognize a bird's distress or alarm call, you will be able to rescue many birds. If a cat, snake, or owl is near, a bird gives its alarm call. If it is caught so that it cannot free itself, it will also call.

Sometimes, when a bird is carrying nesting materials, a long string or thread may catch on a branch or wire and jerk the bird in such a way that it becomes hopelessly entangled. Children have often rescued birds that were hanging from branches or wires by a long string or thread. Sometimes these children find birds whose feet are entangled in hair that was removed from a comb and thrown outdoors.

One hummingbird was held fast in the web of a big yellow and black garden spider, which had spun so many threads about it that the poor little bird could not even move a wing. This extra webbing was so strong that scissors were needed to remove it from the bird.

The distress call of blue jays disclosed the fact that a large blacksnake had climbed a tree and was about to devour a young jay. It had already swallowed one **nestling**, but the other three were rescued.

Sometimes during migration, a bird becomes exhausted and must fly down and rest. A boy saw a tired **coot**—a small, ducklike bird that lives in marshes and has long, rounded toes instead of webs—on the pavement in a large city. He gave it

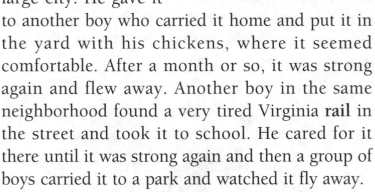

Bald Coot

to another boy who carried it home and put it in the yard with his chickens, where it seemed comfortable. After a month or so, it was strong again and flew away. Another boy in the same neighborhood found a very tired Virginia **rail** in the street and took it to school. He cared for it there until it was strong again and then a group of boys carried it to a park and watched it fly away.

If you train your eyes and ears to see and hear things as you walk along, you can do much good by rescuing birds in distress.

Review

1. How should you approach birds to study them?

2. Where is the best place to observe birds?

3. How can you see a bird's true colors?

4. What accidents happen to birds during the nesting season?

Some Things To Do

Practice kissing the back of your hand or whistling to coax a bird to answer you. Birds' calls can be heard on special recordings found in the library or on most multimedia versions of encyclopedias on CD-ROM.

If you see a long piece of string or thread outdoors, cut or break it into very short lengths so that the birds can carry it more easily and safely. Be on the alert to rescue birds, but be sure to wear gloves to protect you from any disease they may carry.

Black Skimmer

Chapter Four

Insects

The Wasp

Listen to that buzzing! It does not sound like a bee. It is a wasp working on its nest. There are many kinds of wasps; some are black with purple and steel-blue wings, and some are brown with yellow markings and **iridescent** wings—wings that show the colors of the rainbow. The wings do not have scales like the butterflies' wings, or wing covers like the beetles' wings. A wasp seems to jerk its wings constantly, but when it rests they fold together over its back.

Fastened to the wasp's head are two jointed feelers that curve outward. One is called an antenna; both are called antennae. It has two large eyes. That part of its body behind its head is called the **thorax**; to it are fastened the wasp's four wings and six legs. The **abdomen** is joined to the thorax by a long, slim, threadlike waist, and the stinger is at the rear end of the abdomen.

Head   Thorax   Abdomen

When observing a wasp, it is best not to get too near it; and if a person remains quiet, a wasp may alight on him without stinging. If anyone is stung, moist clay, or a slice of raw onion, should be applied at once. Either remedy will prevent the swelling and pain that result from a sting.

It is interesting to watch a wasp exploring for a nesting site. Once a mud dauber wasp, exploring the corner of a shed, examined every inch of the boards with its antennae, flew around and around as though it were getting landmarks so it could find the same place again, and then flew away. Soon it returned with a tiny ball of mud, shaped like a pellet, which it carried against its mouth and supported with its front feet. The wasp had chewed the mud until it was thoroughly mixed with the saliva in its mouth before it formed the little pellet, which would then be very hard and strong when dry. It alighted on the wall in the corner, pressed the pellet against the board, and began to hum loudly. As the wasp hummed, it spread the pellet round and round, using its head and front feet as a trowel is used. Then it flew away to get another pellet.

The wasp returned to the shed and spread this pellet out, humming and moving its wings a little as it worked, making a flat **foundation**, or base, for its nest. Perhaps the **vibration**, or rapid movement, of its wings caused the loud humming sound. It had to make many trips to the mud puddle, for it could carry only one little pellet at a time.

When the wasp had completed the foundation, it began to make a cell by spreading out a pellet and curving it upward as it worked. Then the wasp used three pellets to make a ring overlapping this. It continued in this manner until it had fifteen rings neatly overlapping each other, and all touching the foundation. The whole cell looked like a tube of mud with its side fastened to the foundation, and one end left open. Inside, it was about an inch long and three eighths of an inch wide, and it was smooth; but on the outside, every ring showed. It was beautifully made.

Then the wasp began to make another cell beside the first one, each ring touching the foundation and also the first cell. When this was half finished, the wasp carried a spider and packed it into the end of the first cell in such a way that it

NATURE READER BOOK 4

did not fall out. Altogether, the wasp packed twenty-three spiders into that cell, and then laid an egg on one of the spiders. The egg was white with a yellow dot and about the size of the head of a common pin. Then the mother wasp brought a mud pellet and began to close the first cell, using several pellets to seal it.

If one learns to recognize the humming of a busy wasp, he may often see it working. It usually builds several mud cells, fills them with spiders, places an egg in each cell, and seals them. Then the wasp plasters mud over them all to make it look like a mud ball thrown against the wall.

The wasp not only has to make good use of its sharp eyes, but must also be brave to catch a spider, because spiders like to eat wasps. Early one morning, a wasp flew to a spider's web in a bush. The spider was out on its web and the wasp flew back and forth, this way and that way, in front of it. The wasp flew so near the web without touching it that every moment it looked as though the wasp would become entangled in the web. All the while the spider watched every movement the wasp made. Suddenly, the wasp seized the spider, quickly bent itself double, and stung it. Do you see how the wasp's threadlike waist helped it? That sting **paralyzed** the spider; it was alive but could not move. Then the wasp carried the spider through the air to its cell.

Things do not always work out as planned for a wasp because sometimes the spider is quick to spin out a thread and entangle the wasp. The little spider may win, even though the wasp puts up a hard fight, and finally may succeed in enclosing the entire wasp in a web case.

A tiny larva hatches from the wasp egg and eats the spiders that are in its cell. It is dark in the cell, but that does not matter, for the larva's work is to eat and grow. When it has feasted on all the spiders, it is soft, white with a yellow head, very plump, and just large enough to fit in its cell. Then it weaves a little silken cocoon about itself and rests, while a wonderful change occurs. It becomes a new creature, called a pupa, and is helpless until another change occurs. Its case or covering splits along the back, and discloses a beautiful winged creature—a wasp. It is noisy as it spits out saliva to soften the end of its cell, and chews its way out. Then it flies away. Is it not wonderful that its head is right at the end of its cell so that it can eat its way out?

Adult Pupa Larva Egg

Some wasps burrow tunnels in the ground and **excavate**, or dig, little cells. They sting a large caterpillar to place in each cell with the egg, and the wasp larva feeds upon the caterpillar, which is still alive but paralyzed. Once a wasp carried a large green caterpillar to its burrow. After it had stung the caterpillar, the wasp straddled it and caught hold of it behind the head, and flew low, the rear end of the caterpillar dragging along on the ground. This shows how very strong a wasp must be to carry such a large caterpillar as it flies.

Sometimes a wasp will hunt for a **cicada**, sting it, straddle it, climb up a tree trunk carrying it along, and then

Cicada

glide down through the air to the place where its burrow is in the ground. This performance is very interesting to observe. Some wasps place a large grasshopper in each cell with the egg instead of using a caterpillar, a cicada, a cricket, spiders, or flies. The wasp always stings its victim before it attempts to carry it away to the cell. Some wasps use keyholes for their cells and plaster them up with mud, while others use knotholes in trees.

Some wasps chew old wood to form pellets, which are used to make a nest of many cells. The cells are arranged like the cells in a honeycomb but look like gray paper. It is interesting to watch a wasp getting decayed wood from an old log in the woods and to see how busy the creature is about its work of chewing the tiny bits—not paying any attention to anything or anybody. As the wasp flies away, it holds the tiny gray ball, or pellet, against its mouth with its front feet. When it reaches its nesting site, it spreads out the tiny pellet, gluing it firmly to the wood as it works with its head and front feet. While working, its wings vibrate, making a humming sound. After it has glued a paper foundation to the wood, the wasp begins to form a strong stem downward from the center of it. Of course, the wasp uses many little gray pellets to do this part of the work. When the stem is nearly an inch in length, it is made wider at the bottom, and then work is begun on the paper cells. Each cell is six-sided, like the cell in a honeycomb, about one-fourth inch in diameter and made of beautiful gray paper. These wasps do not finish one cell before beginning another, but start several before they hunt spiders to place in the first one. A beautifully rounded lid or cover is made to seal the cell after it is filled with spiders and the egg has been deposited in it. Every part of the nest is waterproof, and the weather cannot damage it.

The hornet makes a much more elaborate nest, enclosing it with several layers of paper with air spaces between them.

Hornet

Near one nest of five unfinished cells, a little spider crawled out from its hiding place in a corner of the ceiling of the shed and spun out a web to cover the wasp's nest. Then the spider returned to its hiding place

Nest of Hornets

and waited. After a while the wasp came flying into the shed, carrying its tiny gray pellet, and heading straight for the nest. It must have been excited and in a hurry, for it did not even notice the web enclosing the nest until its feet were entangled in it. How angrily it buzzed! Of course, this brought the spider to investigate the identity of its victim. After advancing a little distance, it seemed to hesitate and then returned to its hiding place. Evidently it must have known that it would require a hard fight to capture that wasp. The

spider advanced and hesitated
three times, and then it
seemed to pick up courage,
for it advanced boldly to
within a little distance of the
wasp and spun out threads.
Finally, it entangled a wing in these
new threads, then one leg, and so on.
One by one, every leg and wing became
entangled, while the wasp fought hard to get out,
even doubling its body up and hurling itself
toward the spider, so that the plucky spider had
to do much dodging to escape the deadly sting of
the wasp. It was a bitter struggle, but the spider
finally had every leg and wing of its victim bound
with threads. Then it spun out quite a number of
threads and crawled back into its hiding place,
pulling the helpless wasp after it. That particular
wasp nest was never finished, though it is not
known whether or not the little spider trapped
any more wasps.

Sometimes a tiny jug-shaped mud cell is found
fastened to the stem of a purple aster in the
woods. This beautiful
little clay jug is
three-eighths of an
inch in diameter, and has
a tiny round hole in one

side where the new wasp has eaten its way out. Nests like it are made by the jug-builder, or potter wasp, which stores small live caterpillars in its little clay jug, and suspends its egg from the ceiling by a tiny silken thread. Several of these pretty little clay jugs may be seen on one stem of a plant in the woods.

A teacher once kept a number of insects in a large screen cage at school. One day the class discovered that the **praying mantis** had seized a wasp in its jawlike front legs, ready to devour it, when the wasp doubled its body and stung the mantis. Both were dead when found—the wasp's stinger **imbedded** in the mantis, and the wasp held in a tight grip by the spines on the jawlike front legs of the mantis. No one, however, had observed the battle. It is very interesting to study a wasp, to see how well it is fitted to carry on its work and to notice how industrious it is.

Praying Mantis

Review

1. Name the three main body parts of a wasp.

2. How does the mud dauber wasp make its nest?

3. How do some other wasps make their nests?

4. What are the four stages of a wasp's life?

Some Things To Do

If you and your teacher find a wasp nest, place it in a screen cage. Watch the wasps emerge. Feed them sweetened water and watch them drink. Notice the position of their legs, antennae, and wings, as they fly. Notice whether the wasp runs along first, or takes to the air at once when it begins to fly. Watch a wasp alight to see whether or not it can stop its flight.

The Bumblebee

Sometimes one sees a large, noisy bee flying from blossom to blossom in a field of beautiful red clover. That is a bumblebee. This stout, inch-long insect is the only bee that is **native** to North America. It has black and yellow stripes that make up its plush coat. Its two short feelers are never quiet, but are always active. It has three simple eyes between its two large **compound**

eyes. If examined through a magnifying glass, the compound eye looks like a honeycomb; it is made up of many small eyes forming one big eye. The bumblebee has a wonderful mouth, also, with which it can bite as well as suck its food.

That part of an insect's body behind its head is called its thorax. The bumblebee has six legs and four wings, which are joined to the thorax. Its wings are strong and look like those of wasps and flies. Its legs are black, jointed, rough, and hairy, and at the end of each leg is a little foot with three joints and a claw. In each hind leg there is a little pocket or basket for pollen. Sometimes the bee may be seen on a flower, filling its baskets with the fine yellow dust called pollen. It is interesting to watch how skillfully it uses its legs to push the pollen into the baskets, for it packs them full before it flies to its nest.

The abdomen is that part of an insect's body behind the thorax. The bumblebee's abdomen is furry and has a stinger at the end of it. A bumblebee never leaves a flower head first, but always comes from it backward, for its weapon of defense, or stinger, is on the end of its abdomen.

Only the mothers, the queen bumblebees, survive the winter. In the fall, a queen will find a crevice or some snug place where the frost and dampness cannot reach her, and there she **hibernates**, or sleeps all winter. In early spring, she flies low over the fields looking for a place to

begin her nest. She prefers the old burrow of a field mouse or a **mole** and works hard arranging the dry grass in it to suit her.

It is interesting to watch a bumblebee that is about to make her nest and see how carefully she examines every inch of the region around the entrance so she can find it again. The first flight from her new home is very important, for she must get her bearings in order to find her way back to it. She comes out, crawls all around the entrance, takes wing slowly as she faces it, and then flies in circles, getting a little farther from it each time until she makes a large circle, and then away she goes. After a few trips, she will fly directly to and from the nest. Her sense of direction is wonderful.

The queen bumblebee works hard, filling her baskets with pollen and getting nectar from flowers. The pollen is like fine yellow dust, and sometimes, when you smell a flower, it gets on your nose. She mixes the pollen and nectar to make **beebread** and places it in a hole or cavity in the dry grass in her nest. When she has a loaf about as large as a bean, she lays tiny eggs on it and covers all with wax.

She provides for bad weather by making a little wax pot, about as large as a thimble, somewhere near the beebread and eggs. She fills this with honey to eat while she broods over her eggs to keep them warm. The honey she makes, though, is not pleasant to eat. When the larvae hatch, they eat the beebread.

The bumblebee larvae, or grubs, are smooth and white and have no legs. When the little grubs are full-grown, they spin a cocoon about themselves and change into pupae. Then they change again and become winged creatures and eat their way out of their cocoons. Most adult bumblebees are female workers which are a little smaller than their queen mother, but they cannot lay eggs.

After **metamorphosis**, all these grubs become full-grown workers that immediately begin to take care of the growing family. The queen remains in the nest and continues her work of laying eggs, while the workers go out to gather pollen and nectar from flowers, make beebread and wax, and feed the grubs. After a grub becomes a bee, the workers strengthen its cocoon with wax and fill it with honey.

Every egg in a bumblebee's nest in spring and early summer becomes a worker, or sister bee. Late in the summer, however, the queen bumblebee lays eggs that become drones and young queens. The drones are the brother bees and do no work at all. They are the mates for the new queens. When the weather gets cold in the fall, the workers and drones get sleepy and die, but the queens search for a snug place to spend the winter and will awake in the spring to make new nests.

Bumblebees carry pollen for thousands of flowers, especially red clover blossoms, which helps the farmers. Other bees cannot carry the red clover pollen because their tongues are not long enough to reach the nectar. The red clover does not produce a good crop of seeds unless there are bumblebees to carry its pollen. We should not harm a bumblebee, especially a worker or queen.

Review

1. Where do bumblebees nest?

2. What becomes of them in winter?

3. Of what use are bumblebees to farmers?

Some Things To Do

From a safe distance, watch a bumblebee at work among the flowers. Notice which flowers it visits, and whether or not it passes by some of them. Notice how it enters and leaves a flower.

The Ladybug

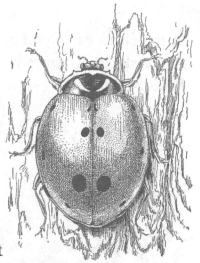

Although there are many kinds of ladybugs, they all resemble a hard, shiny pill cut in half, with legs joined to the flat underside. Some are dark red or yellow with black spots, and others are black with red or yellow spots, but all are neat and clean. The ladybug is a beetle, with hard, shiny wing covers that meet in a straight line down the middle of its back;

these wing covers usually have spots on them. The ladybug's antennae, or feelers, are short and like little clubs. The part of its body behind the head is called the thorax. The ladybug's thorax has spots on it and a colored shield to protect it. The six little legs are black, like the underside of its body. The long, thin, delicate wings are folded under the wing covers when the ladybug is not flying, but sometimes it runs along with the tips of its wings hanging out.

If one touches a ladybug, it will pretend that it is dead. It will fold up its little legs, drop down, and lie quietly on its back for a couple of minutes. Then it will kick with its six little legs and turn over again, ready to crawl away.

In spring, the ladybug lays its eggs on plants where there are aphids, **scale insects**, or **mealybugs**. Aphids are plant lice that do much damage by sucking the sap of plants. Scale insects and mealybugs also suck the sap of plants, doing much harm to vegetation. When the ladybug larva hatches from the egg, it runs about searching for these insects to eat.

The ladybug larva is an odd-looking creature with a long body divided into segments. Its "coat" is usually black with orange spots and looks like velvet. It has little bumps or warts on each segment. Its six short, little legs help it crawl quite rapidly, and it does nothing but crawl around on plants and eat aphids, scale insects, and mealybugs. It gobbles up these insects every day until it is full-grown; it is surprising how many it eats. As the larva grows, it sheds its skin, like a caterpillar. Each time it **molts**, or sheds its skin, the new skin is larger than the old; and it must shed its old skin to accommodate its growth. When the larva is full-grown, it seeks a quiet corner, sometimes on a twig, hangs itself by the tail, and rests.

Now a wonderful change occurs. Its old skin bursts and is pushed forward, disclosing a new creature called the pupa. After a few days, the skin of the pupa bursts, and out crawls a beautiful ladybug. It flies about seeking a place to spend the winter. It may enter a home to hide, or it may

crawl beneath leaves or pine needles, or beneath loose pieces of bark on a tree, where it will be protected from the severe storms of winter. Sometimes one can see them beneath loose bark on trees in city parks.

Ladybugs are very helpful insects; the gardeners of Europe and North America have known this for a long time, and they never harm one. They are always glad when they discover these little beetles on their plants, for they realize how many harmful insects the larvae destroy in a season.

The Australian ladybug saved California's orange trees that were being destroyed by scale insects. Another kind of ladybug saved the cantaloupe vines there when aphids were destroying them. Without healthy trees and vines, it is impossible to produce good crops of delicious fruits and melons. Ladybugs help to keep them healthy by eating the insects which destroy them.

If aphids, or plant lice, are seen on the rose bushes in the yard in June, ladybugs will soon be busy laying their eggs on the leaves. It is interesting, then, to see how the larvae eat the plant lice. Never harm a ladybug, and, if one enters the house, either let it alone or put it outdoors again.

Review

1. How can you recognize a ladybug when you see one?

2. Describe its larva.

3. How does it help the gardener?

4. Why should we never harm ladybugs?

Some Things To Do

Watch a ladybug crawl and fly. Find a twig with aphids and a ladybug larva on it. Watch how the larva destroys the aphids. Keep the twig just one day, and then place the larva on a plant outdoors where there are aphids.

Aphids

Aphids are the small insects, called plant lice, which are often seen on flowers and bushes. Most aphids are green, like the stems and young leaves of plants, but some are brownish. All are small and have soft, plump bodies with two antennae and six legs. Usually they do not have wings.

Their sucking tube is folded back beneath their bodies as they crawl along and pat the stem with their antennae to feel their way. They are not bothered about their neighbors and even crawl over other aphids to find a place that suits them. When they find such a place, they thrust their sucking tube into the stem or leaf and drink the sap. Usually all aphids on a stem have their heads in the same direction.

In summer, only "female" aphids are born alive— none are hatched from eggs. If one looks closely at a potted plant on which some aphids live, he will see what appear to be tiny bits of white lint on the soil or leaves; these are baby aphids. When there are too many aphids on one plant, some are born with wings; these will fly away, sailing on the breeze, to seek their food on other plants. In the fall, both male and true female aphids are found on plants. These females lay eggs which hatch into "female" aphids the following spring.

When ants are seen crawling up and down  plant stems, one should look for aphids. An ant will crawl up to an aphid, gently stroke it with its antennae, and then drink the liquid from it. This liquid is sweet and is called **honeydew**. Because ants do this, these aphids are called "ant cows," for the ants "milk" them to get the honeydew. Ants are very fond of this honeydew, and they care for aphids and protect them in order to get this sweet liquid. They will carry the eggs of certain aphids down into their own burrows for the winter and then place the baby aphids on the roots of plants in the spring.

Aphids

Some aphids suck the sap of tender leaves and stems, while others feed on the roots of certain plants; but all of them suck the sap of plants, instead of eating parts of them, and that does much damage. A poisonous spray usually does not affect them, because they do not eat any of the poison; but a spray made with tobacco extract will kill aphids when it touches their bodies. The best spray is a mixture of a spoonful of tobacco extract and a little soap added to one gallon of water.

Moreover, aphids have some natural enemies which will keep them in check. One enemy is the aphid lion, a little **spindle-shaped** larva with jaws

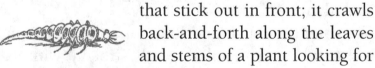

that stick out in front; it crawls back-and-forth along the leaves and stems of a plant looking for prey. When it finds an aphid, it loses no time in sucking out all the aphid's body fluids and is soon ready for another victim.

Another enemy of aphids is the ladybug larva. This little larva does not look at all like the trim little beetle it will become. It is long, with velvety rings of black with orange and yellow spots, a rough back, and six short legs. It also hunts aphids and gobbles them up.

A third enemy is a tiny four-winged fly that lays its eggs on aphids. When the eggs hatch, the larvae eat the aphids.

The aphid has two little tubes on the end of its body. When an enemy approaches, it shoots out tiny drops from the tubes into its enemy's face. These drops are liquid and harden like wax when dry, forcing the enemy to stop and clean its face before it can attack.

Learn to recognize the aphid lion and the ladybug larva so you will not make the mistake of destroying two insects that help us by eating aphids.

Review

1. How can you tell when aphids are on a plant?

2. How do aphids harm plants?

3. How do aphids and ants work together?

4. What are some of the aphid's natural enemies?

5. How can we destroy aphids?

Some Things To Do

Find a twig with aphids on it. Observe how they move and how they eat. Place the twig in a tight cage and put several ants in it also. Observe how the ants behave toward the aphids.

The Lacewing

The lacewing is a small insect, so delicate and dainty that it reminds one of a fairy. It is as green as a new leaf, and its wings are lacy and iridescent—showing the dainty rainbow colors. Its eyes are golden, its antennae, or feelers, are quite long, and it has six green legs. Birds do not eat it, for the lacewing gives off a bad odor which protects it from its enemies; this is why it is sometimes called a "stinkfly."

It flies about looking for a plant or tree which has many aphids on it. Do you remember what the aphids do? These aphids, or plant lice, do much damage by sucking the sap of leaves and stems of plants. The lacewing alights on a leaf; spins a stiff, threadlike stalk about half an inch long; and places a tiny long egg at the very tip of it. Several of these silky stalks with glistening eggs at their tips may be seen on one leaf; from a distance,  they might be mistaken for mold on the leaf. Do you know why these tiny eggs are at the tips of little threadlike stalks, instead of being flat on the leaf like other insects' eggs? This prevents the larvae from eating the unhatched eggs.

If one watches the eggs daily, he will see a wonderful thing happen. The eggs begin to look dark and soon little creatures eat their way out and cling to their shells with their six little claws. They hold on tight as they crawl about. Finally, the larvae gain courage, climb down their stalks to the leaf, and scurry away in search of aphids.

This little creature is very unusual. Its body is shaped like a spindle, and it has two long, curved jaws sticking out from its head. Its six little legs help it run fast. It seizes an aphid with its sickle-shaped jaws, holds it up in the air, then sucks its body fluids. The larva eats many aphids before it becomes a pupa. It grows, like other insects, by shedding its skin. When the larva is full-grown, it fastens itself to a leaf and spins a tiny white silk cocoon, which looks like a beautiful little pearl. Inside this cocoon, it changes to a pupa and is helpless while it rests. Later it changes into a beautiful, green, lacy-winged creature with golden eyes. It then emerges from its cocoon and flies away.

We should never harm a lacewing, because it lays eggs which become the larvae, or aphid lions, that destroy aphids.

Review

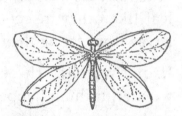

1. Describe a lacewing.
2. Give the life history of the aphid lion.
3. Why should we protect the lacewing?

Some Things To Do

Look for lacewing eggs on leaves of a plant. Take the eggs home and observe them every day to see them hatch. Watch to see what happens when the aphid lions are placed on a plant or twig that has some aphids. The next day, place the aphid lions back on the same plant where you found the eggs.

Look up the lacewing in the encyclopedia and find out more about these interesting insects. Perhaps you could find some books in the library about them, too.

The Mosquito

If one looks into a rain barrel, he may see little wigglers in the water. Down they sink out of sight, and then they come up again, hanging head downward in the water. They are the larvae of mosquitoes. These larvae are also called wiggle-tails.

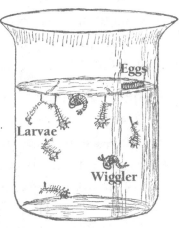

At first there is a black spot like soot on the water. This is the egg case of about three hundred tiny eggs fastened to one another. It floats so well that, if pushed down, it bobs to the top again and seems as dry as before.

A young wiggler hatches out of the bottom of its egg in a day or two and sinks in the rain water. The wiggler's head and thorax—the part behind its head—are quite large, but its body gradually **tapers**, or becomes smaller, toward its tail. It has tufts of hair on each segment of its body; and, at the tail end of its body, there are two unusual little tubes.

One of these tubes is long and straight; it is the breathing tube. At its tip is a valve which can be opened and closed. When it is opened at the surface of the water, it keeps the wiggler afloat and lets air pass into its body. When disturbed, the wiggler closes the valve and sinks. The other tube helps it swim and has four little swimming organs and tufts of hair.

When the wiggler swims, it goes tail first in jerks. It reminds one of an acrobat. It reaches the surface of the water, opens the valve in its breathing tube, and rests head downward at an angle of about forty-five degrees. While hanging like this, it feeds on tiny bits of decaying vegetation. It moves the brushes, or tufts of hair, on its jaws so rapidly that the food is brought to its mouth. Sometimes it feeds at the bottom of the water, but only for a moment, because it must have fresh air often.

Wigglers

As a wiggler grows, it sheds its skin; and in a few days it is full-grown, changes into a pupa, and rests head upward in the water. The pupa's head and thorax are very large but its body is small. It breathes through the little tubes in its thorax. At the end of its body are the swimming organs that look like two little leaves; but the pupa does not swim much unless it is disturbed.

If the weather is warm, another change takes place in about two days. The pupa rises to the surface of the water, its skin bursts, and out crawls a wet, brownish creature with wrinkled wings. It clings to the old skin of the pupa until it is dry and its wings are strong. It is a mosquito, and is now ready to fly.

Eggs

Larva

Pupa

Adult

The mosquito's eyes, like those of other insects, are very large. If its eye is examined under a microscope, it looks like a honeycomb, for many small eyes form it. The male mosquito's antennae are like feathers and help him hear his mate's song. The female's antennae are plain. Did you ever hear a mosquito sing? We think its song is made by the rapid vibration of its wings. Only the female mosquito can sing and bite; it sings to attract its mate.

The male mosquito feeds upon the nectar of flowers. The female has a long, hard, slender organ like a tube and lance; she uses this to pierce our skin and suck our blood. Some of her saliva enters the skin when she bites us, causing the bitten area to swell and itch. Certain mosquitoes with spotted wings carry **malaria**; others carry **yellow fever** and other diseases.

During the day, mosquitoes hide under the leaves of bushes until late in the afternoon when they fly about in search of food; and they often get into people's houses. To control these pests, **insecticides**—chemicals used to kill insects—are sometimes used to spray door and window screens. Because mosquitoes breed in water, many can be destroyed by emptying or draining pools and ponds. If a pond is stocked with goldfish or minnows, they will feed on the wigglers and pupae of the mosquitoes. If bats are protected and birds attracted to where mosquitoes live, they will also help in keeping mosquitoes in check.

There is a large brown insect which closely resembles a mosquito but does not bite. It is the **crane fly**. The crane fly may be very small or grow to be over an inch long. This slow-flying insect is harmless to people and is usually found around water or among many plants. The crane fly deposits its small, black eggs in damp areas. Each egg hatches into a long, slender larva which is named a "leatherjacket" after its tough, brown skin. They usually feed on decaying plants; but some eat other insects, while others damage the roots of crops. The larvae feed all winter, then enter a resting stage in the spring.

Review

1. Give the life history of the mosquito.

2. What are the natural enemies of a mosquito?

3. How can mosquitoes be controlled?

Some Things To Do

Find some wiggle-tails and put them in a glass of rain water. Fasten a piece of netting over the top of the glass with a rubber band. Observe them each day to note changes in their appearance and actions. Disturb the water to see what happens. Put a few of them in the aquarium with the goldfish. Watch to see what happens.

The Dragonfly and Damselfly

Let us watch that large beautiful insect darting back-and-forth above the pond. It flies across the fields. How fast it goes! It makes one think of an airplane. See how quickly it turns in any direction! Now it is actually flying backward. It is a dragonfly.

There are several kinds of dragonflies. Nearly all of them have metallic colors; that is, they glisten in the sunlight. Some have beautiful rainbow colors, and one kind is gorgeous in its "coat" of metallic green. Its body is very long and rather slender. Its four pretty wings are smooth and clear, like a wasp's or fly's wings, and are sometimes beautifully spotted. These powerful wings are strengthened by heavy veins.

The dragonfly's two large compound eyes make up about two-thirds of its head. If an insect's compound eye is magnified, it looks like a piece of honeycomb; it is really many little eyes forming one big eye. The compound eye of a dragonfly shows beautiful colors as one looks at it. The dragonfly also has little simple eyes in the front of

its head. Its sight is very keen; it can see not only far away, but near itself, too. Its head is joined to its body in such a way that it can see above, beneath, and in front of itself. The dragonfly's antennae are very short; it does not need long ones because of its wonderful sight.

As you have learned, every insect's body may be divided into three parts—the head; the thorax, to which the legs and wings are attached; and the abdomen. The dragonfly's six legs and four strong wings are attached to its stout thorax. Its abdomen is very long and slender. It uses its six legs like a basket to catch insects while flying, and loses no time in doing it. It devours so many mosquitoes, gnats, and flies that it is said to be **voracious**, or greedy in eating; some people call it the "mosquito hawk." Dragonflies are busy on a sunny day, but are seldom seen when it is cloudy.

The dragonfly lays its eggs in the water of a pond or stream. These eggs sink to the bottom and hatch into little larvae called **nymphs**. The nymph is a very peculiar-looking creature that lives in the water. All **aquatic** insects are interesting, but the nymph of the dragonfly is especially so. It is greenish-gray and remains quiet on the bed of the pond or stream, hiding in the mud and slime. Its body is thick, its head is large, and its mouth is different from those of other insects. Its lower lip is a horny plate covering the underside of its head and

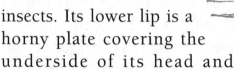

Dragonfly Larva

extending back under its two front legs. We call this horny plate its mask, because it covers the lower part of the nymph's head. When an aquatic insect comes near it, the nymph unfolds its mask and shoots out two little pincerlike jaws that seize the insect and draw it into its mouth with lightning speed. Then the nymph chews and swallows its prey, folds its mask, and is ready for the next victim. It attacks and devours any aquatic insect, even some that are larger than itself. It may even eat the eyes out of a minnow.

Though the dragonfly nymph is very **ferocious**, or extremely cruel, it has many enemies. Catfish, crappie, pickerel, sunfish, bass, and other fish feed on the nymphs. Large aquatic insects, like the diving beetles, devour them, too. Larger dragonfly nymphs will even eat smaller nymphs.

Dragonfly nymphs move slowly and look like the mud and slime at the bottom of the pond or stream where they live; because of this, other aquatic insects cannot see them until it is too late to escape their fierce jaws. Though the nymph has six legs, it moves along by drawing in and forcing out drafts of water through its intestinal tracts. It does this with such force that it is actually pushed ahead through the water.

As the nymph grows, it sheds its skin, or molts. After each molt, it is more ferocious than before. After molting ten or eleven times, its head is larger, and little bumps, or wing pads, appear on its back. Each time it molts, these bumps grow larger until they **protrude**, or stand out, from its body when the nymph is full-grown. Then, early in the morning, it crawls up the stem of a plant until it is above the water. It fastens its claws firmly into the stem, its skin splits along the back, and out crawls a gorgeous winged creature with a very long, slender body—a dragonfly. It holds tight while the air and sun harden its legs. Its wings expand and harden, its body becomes stronger, and then away it flies to hunt for insects to devour.

Often you will see dainty insects resembling dragonflies near streams and ponds. They are damselflies. Their bodies are more slender and more beautifully colored than the dragonflies', many of them being iridescent green, or coppery.

The damselfly's eyes are on the sides of its head and are not as large as those of the dragonfly. It also is not as strong a flier as the dragonfly, for its wings are smaller and less powerful. It usually flies low over the water and often stops to rest, folding its wings vertically over its back. When the dragonfly rests, however, its wings are out, as in flight.

Nymph of the Damselfly

The damselfly cuts a slit in the stem of an aquatic plant and lays its eggs in the opening. The nymphs hatch and live in the water, feeding on aquatic insects. Their habits are much like those of the dragonfly nymphs. Both have a large lower lip like a mask, and both attack minnows and devour aquatic insects. The damselfly nymph is longer than the dragonfly nymph and has three leaflike **gills** at the end of its body. These gills aid it in breathing and swimming. When the nymph is full-grown, it climbs up the stem of an aquatic plant, or crawls out on the bank, and becomes a winged creature called the damselfly.

Formerly, some people believed that dragonflies helped snakes, and called them "snake doctors." Some folks even thought they stung horses. The truth of the matter is that they are harmless and do not sting at all. They are very useful to people and horses, because they destroy countless numbers of insects that bite or sting. Watch dragonflies and damselflies, but never harm them. If one should fly into the house, help it find its way outdoors again, but do not hurt it.

Review

1. Why is the dragonfly called a "mosquito hawk"?

2. What does the dragonfly nymph use to get its food easily?

3. What is the difference between a dragonfly and a damselfly?

4. Why should we never harm a dragonfly or damselfly?

Some Things To Do

Watch a dragonfly and compare its flight with that of a butterfly. Scoop up some water and mud from a pond to see if you can get a nymph of the dragonfly or damselfly. Observe it carefully and then put it back into the pond.

GOD, WHO MADE THE EARTH

God who made the earth, The air, the sky, the

sea, Who gave the light its birth, Car-eth for me.

Chapter Five
Moths

The Tomato Hornworm

If you have a tomato plant in your yard, you can expect to find tomato hornworms eating its leaves; these "worms" have tiny hornlike tips at the end of their abdomens, which give them their name. They are really caterpillars, or larvae, of a particular **sphinx** moth called the "five-spotted hawk moth"—so named because it has five rows of yellow spots on its abdomen and flies about so rapidly. The larvae's light-green color protects them when they rest on a stem or the underside of a leaf. Some tomato hornworms are black instead of green. All grow to be very large caterpillars if nothing happens to them.

At first, the tomato hornworm is an egg that is laid by a female moth on the underside of a leaf on the tomato plant. When the tiny caterpillar hatches, it eats this leaf. It has an enormous appetite, for it eats leaves greedily until its

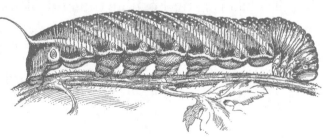

skin becomes too tight. Then it is quiet and does not eat for a while. Soon its skin splits down the back, and out crawls the caterpillar in a bright new coat. You can even see it lift out each leg and push the old skin backward as it crawls out. Then the wrinkled old skin falls down and the wind blows it away. The larva is larger now, and its new skin is beautiful. When it sheds its old skin, we say that a caterpillar molts. This is how all caterpillars grow. After resting a while, it begins to eat leaves again and is soon ready to molt a second time. It does this until it is full-grown.

Look at the big caterpillar closely, and you will see that it is green like the stems and leaves of the tomato plant, with little white stripes on its sides. The tiny holes along its sides are the **spiracles**, or holes, through which it breathes, since it has no nostrils and does not breathe through its mouth.

Touch the caterpillar gently to see how it raises the front of its body, draws in its head, stiffens itself or becomes rigid, and tries to frighten you; it also has a little horn at the end of its body that will not sting or hurt you. Its appearance, however, probably does frighten some of its enemies. That is why it is called a sphinx caterpillar.

The caterpillar's six front legs are its true legs. They are short, and have little sharp claws for grasping and holding a leaf while the caterpillar eats it. Watch it eat to see how its jaws move sideways. Its eight thick, or fleshy, legs are its **prolegs**; and the large, fleshy one at the end of its body is its prop leg. Caterpillars and some other larvae have extra sets of "legs," called prolegs, which are attached to their abdomens; these prolegs are different from their true legs, which are attached to their thoraxes. Each proleg has a tiny disk or vacuum cup to help it get a firm grip and hold tight. Since the caterpillar is nearsighted, it crawls to another leaf by holding tight with its prolegs and prop leg as it reaches far out with its true legs. When it touches another leaf, it grasps this with its true legs and then lifts its prolegs and prop leg, drawing itself up on the new leaf. The caterpillar begins to eat this leaf and then crawls to other leaves and eats them, until it is full-grown.

When full-grown, the caterpillar quits eating, crawls down to the ground, and is very restless. It seems to be looking for something, and when it reaches a place where the soil is loose, it gets busy. It works like a steam shovel—down goes its head, up comes the soil. It soon disappears, and you cannot even see where it went down into the ground. It digs down three, four, or five inches;

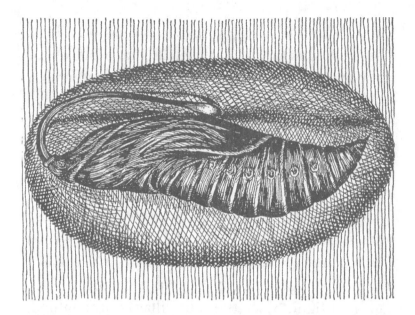

and there makes a nice little **oval-shaped** room that we call a cell. The inside of the cell is smooth dirt pressed tight, making firm walls. The caterpillar goes to sleep, changes into a pupa, or chrysalis, and remains there all winter.

This pupa is a beautiful dark-brown color, long, pointed at one end, and usually has what looks like the handle of a jug at the other end. Looking at it closely, you will see that this "handle" is the case for the antennae of the new moth. You can also see where the head, wings, **segments** or rings, and the spiracles are. The cold weather, snow, and ice do not hurt the pupa; and in spring, it becomes a beautiful large, grayish moth that crawls up out of the ground and flies away.

A moth is different from a butterfly. A moth's body is thick and furry, but a butterfly has a smooth, slender body. Both insects have two feelers called antennae. A moth's antennae, however, are like little feathers or threads, while those of a butterfly are long and slender with a little knob at the end of each of them.

A sphinx moth's antennae are like slender feathers; and its thick, furry body is grayish with beautiful dots on it. The moth that develops from the tomato hornworm has five or six rows of yellow spots on its abdomen. Other sphinx moths may have rose or red colors on their bodies and wings. The two front wings are much larger than the two back wings, but both pairs are narrow and long. They are grayish and beautifully marked with black or colored lines and spots.

Head of Sphinx Moth

A sphinx moth—sometimes called a hawk moth—comes out just before dark. As it searches for food, it uses its long tongue to reach way down into the center of the morning glory, **moonflower**, **jimson weed**, petunia, and other deep-throated flowers. It visits these flowers in the early evening; and, as it flies from flower to

Sphinx Moth

flower, its long tongue hangs down, ready to sip the nectar from the next flower.

The moth does not have to alight on the flower, like a butterfly does, to get the nectar. The hawk moth keeps its wings moving rapidly and stays in one place as it reaches down into the flower with its long tongue. We say that it hovers near the flower as it sips the nectar. Since it moves its strong wings so rapidly when flying, you can hear them hum; that is why some people call it the "hummingbird moth." If there are many flowers, the moth lets its tongue hang down as it flies from flower to flower getting nectar. When it leaves the group of flowers, it coils its tongue beneath its head like the spring of a watch.

You may see a funny-looking tomato hornworm with little white things on its back. They are shaped like grains of wheat, and are tiny silk cocoons spun by little caterpillars that lived in the tomato hornworm until they were full-grown. Then they crawled out of the tomato hornworm, eating their way through its skin, and spun their tiny cocoons on its back. In each little cocoon there is a tiny pupa that will change into a little four-winged fly. It eats around the top of the cocoon so that it will lift up like a lid; and then the insect crawls out, dries its wings, and flies away. Later, this little insect will look for another tomato hornworm, alight on the worm's back, puncture the skin, and lay its egg right in the worm.

The tomato hornworm with tiny cocoons on its back will die. It cannot live until it is full-grown, and cannot dig its way into the ground; neither can it change into a pupa nor become a beautiful moth. Therefore, we should never destroy the little cocoons on the tomato hornworm's back, for the little four-winged flies, called **parasites**, do much good by destroying the tomato hornworms that eat our plants.

All sphinx caterpillars do not eat tomato leaves as the larvae of the hawk moth eat. Some eat leaves from grape, Virginia creeper, cherry, willow, tobacco, and other plants. For example, the Carolina sphinx moth has larvae, called tobacco hornworms, that are pests of potato, tobacco, and tomato plants.

Review

1. How is the tomato hornworm protected?
2. How does it grow?
3. How does it breathe?
4. Where does it change into a pupa?
5. How can you recognize a sphinx moth?
6. Why is it called a "hawk moth"? A "hummingbird moth"?
7. Why should we not destroy the tiny white cocoons on the backs of these caterpillars?

Some Things To Do

Find a tomato hornworm, or sphinx caterpillar, and some tomato leaves. Watch the caterpillar eat and molt. When it is full-grown, place it on some soil in a narrow, deep, glass case covered with dark paper, and watch it dig down into the soil. After a few days, remove the dark paper to see the cell with the pupa in it. Set it away until spring, and then watch the moth crawl up out of the soil and fly away.

Find a tomato hornworm with tiny white cocoons on its back. Place it in a covered glass case and feed it tomato leaves. Watch the tiny flies come out of the cocoons. Let them go outside so they may hunt other tomato hornworms.

The Cecropia Moth

Have you seen a large cocoon fastened lengthwise on the twig of a shade tree or a fruit tree? Perhaps you wondered at how skillfully it was attached and how strong it was. That was a cecropia cocoon. The giant silkworm that spun and wove the cocoon is the larva of the largest moth in North America. Other large American silkworms are the larvae of the promethea, polyphemus, luna, and cynthia moths; but the larva of the cecropia moth makes the largest cocoon.

The cecropia caterpillar hatches from a tiny brownish-yellow egg, as small as a pin head, that is fastened to the underside of a leaf on a tree, probably a maple or apple tree. At first the baby caterpillar, or larva, is about one-fourth of an inch long. Its business is to eat and grow. This fuzzy, black caterpillar begins eating the leaf on which it was born, and it eats and eats until it is ready to molt, or shed its skin. Then it remains quiet on the underside of a leaf, the skin splits along its back, and it crawls out, pushing the old skin backward just as a boy wiggles out of his swimming suit. Now the larva rests until its new coat is dry. It is larger than before, and its color is a dull orange. It also has tiny black **tubercles**, or little knoblike bumps on its skin.

The cecropia caterpillar begins to eat and, in a few days, 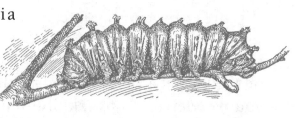 is ready to molt again. Now its new coat is yellow with two large tubercles on the top of each segment; many rings, or segments, make up a caterpillar's body. The tubercles on the first segment are blue, those on the second and third are orange-red, and those on the other segments, except the eleventh, are greenish-blue with black spots and spines. The eleventh segment has one large yellow tubercle bordered with black, but the tubercles along its sides are blue.

The next time the caterpillar molts, its new skin is bluish-green, with large blue tubercles on the top of the first and last segments, orange ones on the second and third, and yellow ones on the others, while those along the side are blue. After molting four times, it becomes a giant caterpillar, as thick as a man's thumb and three or more inches long. No wonder the sparrows let it alone! It is so large and its skin is so tough and elastic that small birds would hardly be able to peck it; in fact, they seem afraid of it. A large cecropia caterpillar will frighten chickens. If it is thrown to them, they will run and make a racket.

It is interesting to watch this giant caterpillar eat, for, like all other larvae, it is nearsighted and never looks beyond the leaf on which it is resting or feeding. Its head is glossy and smooth, and its jaws move sideways. The six front legs are like little claws. They are its true legs and are used to draw the leaf toward its mouth or to hold it steady while eating. The eight fleshy legs are its prolegs and they, together with the prop leg at the end of its body, help it hold tight to wherever it is. If anyone tries to remove the caterpillar from the stem or leaf, he will be surprised to see how tightly it holds.

When ready to eat another leaf, the caterpillar holds tight with its prolegs and prop leg as it lifts the front of its body and reaches out in all directions. When its front or true legs touch another leaf, it gets a grip on it with all six of them and then lifts its prolegs and prop leg and places them somewhere on the new leaf or stem. The caterpillar begins to eat the edge of the leaf, always eating downward, never upward, and it is surprising to see how quickly it can eat a whole leaf. It can sometimes be heard as it chews apple leaves. The caterpillar eats the **midrib** of a leaf last, for it must crawl down the midrib to the twig.

Soon the caterpillar becomes restless and begins to inspect the twig and leaves near it. It covers the entire twig for several inches with silk threads that it spins from its mouth. Then it reaches out, grasps a leaf, draws it toward the twig, and spins silk threads back and forth from the leaf to keep it in place. In the same way, it draws other leaves toward the twig, until it is completely hidden by them. The caterpillar has remarkable endurance; it works its head back and forth, up and down, round and round, spinning out beautiful, light-brown silk threads. Its body gradually grows smaller; in fact, it seems to be shrinking. Finally, the caterpillar has so many threads woven around it that it cannot be seen at all, but can be heard working. At one end, the threads do not cross each other but are laid one way, so that the full-grown moth can more easily leave the cocoon.

When the cocoon is finished, the caterpillar rests inside. Later, it sheds its skin, and is a new creature called a pupa. It is inactive, cannot eat, and is helpless. The short, thick pupa has a smooth skin that is reddish-brown in color. If one examines it carefully, he can see where its eyes, antennae, and wings are forming. The cecropia cocoon will hang on that stout twig all winter and the wind, frost, snow, and ice cannot tear it off or harm it. It is actually rainproof. The pupa is safe in its cocoon unless one of the winter birds pecks a hole in it. The downy woodpecker and the nuthatch are fond of the plump pupa of the cecropia and sometimes parasites destroy the pupa in its cocoon.

These parasites are insects that feed on other living insects. The female parasite alights on a caterpillar's back behind its head, punctures its skin, and lays an egg. This hatches inside the caterpillar and the tiny larva feeds on the tissue of its victim. The caterpillar continues eating as though it does not know that it is being slowly devoured and will never finish its life. It seems that the little larva does not feed on the **vital** parts of its victim and so the caterpillar lives to spin its cocoon and become a pupa. That pupa never becomes a winged creature, for the little larva has destroyed it; but the little parasite becomes a pupa and then a small, winged insect similar to a wasp.

If no bird or parasite destroys the cecropia pupa, it becomes a new creature, forces the threads apart at the end of the cocoon where they were laid one way, and crawls out. It is the most unusual-looking creature! Its body is very large, thick, furry, and wet; its wings are short, wrinkled, thick, and wet, too. It crawls quickly up the side of the cage, if it is in a cage, or merely rests on the twig beside its cocoon if it is in a tree. It holds tight while its body shrinks and dries, and its crumpled wet wings slowly straighten out and expand. Then the moth moves its wings a little to help them dry so it can use them, and soon it flies away.

Cecropia Moth

The cecropia is the largest North American moth, measuring five or six inches across its wings. Its four wings are grayish-brown and have light-colored margins. A broad, white band with a red outer edge crosses each wing. There is a beautiful red spot near the tip of the front wing, near the irregular white line, and a crescent-shaped white spot with a red border in each wing. The moth's antennae are like beautiful reddish feathers, its furry body is striped red and white, and its six furry legs are a reddish-brown. Altogether, it is a pretty creature.

Though the cecropia moth is so large, it does not eat during its short adult life, for its mouth is not fitted to take food. It finds its mate by means of its very strong scent which the antennae help it to detect, lays its eggs on the leaves of a tree that the larvae can eat, and dies. Its work is done.

Review

1. Where are cecropia cocoons found?

2. How is a cecropia cocoon fastened to a twig? Is the pupa safe in its cocoon?

3. How does it happen that parasites emerge from the cocoon?

4. Why does the cecropia moth not eat?

5. Where does it lay its eggs? Why?

Some Things To Do

Find cecropia cocoons and put them in a screen cage. Watch the moths emerge in the spring. Study the moths. If they lay eggs, watch the larvae hatch. Feed the baby larvae apple, mulberry, or maple leaves. Observe them while they eat, molt, and grow. Observe them spin their cocoons. Save these cocoons, and try to **reel** silk from them the following winter. Place one or two moths in a screen cage outdoors. Notice how many moths come to visit your pets during the night.

The Isabella Tiger Moth

When one goes walking in the fall, he may notice a small furry caterpillar crawling along the ground. That is the woolly bear, so named because of its "coat" of thick hair.

The woolly bear is first an egg on a plant such as grass, clover, dandelion, or **plantain**. After crawling out of the egg, the little caterpillar begins to eat the leaf where it was born, as it has nothing to do but eat and grow. As it grows, it sheds its skin, or molts. When it is ready to molt, it quits eating and rests. Then the skin splits along its back, and out comes a bright new caterpillar, pushing the old skin backward as it crawls. It is a little larger than before and rests a while before beginning to eat again.

The woolly bear's back is covered with black or brown bristlelike hairs that are arranged in tiny **rosettes**; these hairs are so short that they look like fur. Its head is black, and its two tiny antennae, or feelers, are yellow. Its eyes are so small that it cannot see very far and must feel its way as it moves along. The caterpillar does this by holding tight with its prolegs and prop leg while it reaches out in every direction to find another leaf. Its six front legs, which are its true legs, have little claws and shine like patent leather. The little claws help the caterpillar reach a leaf and draw it to its mouth when eating. It has eight fleshy legs, called prolegs, and at the end of its body there is a fleshy prop leg. Its prolegs and prop leg help it hold tight to the leaf or stem.

If anyone tries to pick up the woolly bear, it rolls up in a ball and drops to the ground. That is why some people call it the "hedgehog caterpillar." It is not hurt because its hairs are so thick and **elastic**. Those thick elastic hairs also make it hard to pick up the woolly bear when it is curled like a ball.

In the fall, it is full-grown and hurries along to find a snug place to sleep during the winter. In January it may be discovered curled up among the old leaves in a hollow, stump, or among old leaves in a hole in the ground. In the spring it crawls out and begins to eat grass, dandelion leaves, plantain, or other plants.

In April or May, it spins a silk cocoon about itself and weaves in it the hairs from its own body, so that the cocoon looks like felt. Then it becomes a pupa; and in the latter part of May, the pupa becomes a beautiful winged tiger moth that emerges, or comes out, from the cocoon. It crawls up anything near it, so that it can hold tight and let its wet, crumpled wings unfold and expand. Then the moth moves them slowly to help them dry. When they are thoroughly dry, the moth is ready to fly away.

The moth has rows of black dots on its furry body. Its six legs, which are furry, too, are a reddish color tipped with black. Its threadlike antennae are small. It has four beautiful wings arranged in pairs, the front ones being larger than the back ones. The front wings are a grayish-brownish yellow with a few black dots, but the back wings are orange-red. This moth is called a tiger moth because its color is like a tiger's.

Tiger moths fly about at night. During the day they rest—with their wings sloping like a roof over their bodies—on the trunks of trees, rocks, walls, fences, and other places.

The mother moth lays her eggs on the leaves of some plant that the baby caterpillars can eat as soon as they hatch. Some kinds of woolly bears do much harm by eating garden plants and the **foliage** of trees. Since their woolly coats protect them and birds do not like to eat them, their only natural enemies are bats, which eat them at night.

Review

1. How does the woolly bear get its name?
2. How does its "coat" protect it?
3. What are the only natural enemies of the woolly bear caterpillars?

Some Things To Do

Find a woolly bear and some leaves for it to eat. What happens when you pick it up? What does it feel like? Observe how it eats, molts, and spins its cocoon. Observe how the moth emerges.

Isabella Tiger Moth

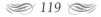

NATURE READER BOOK 4

The Codling Moth

Sometimes one bites into an apple that looks perfect and finds a worm hole or perhaps the worm itself! That worm is the larva of the codling moth. At first this larva is a tiny egg on the young apple or on the new leaves; then it hatches and enters the fruit at the blossom end. It makes a little tunnel as it eats that part of the apple next to the core, and, when it reaches the center, it eats the seeds. It continues to make a little tunnel, eating as it goes, working its way through the pulp to the side of the apple. As the "worm" eats its way, it weaves a thin web in which tiny bits of waste matter may be seen. When it reaches the apple skin, it does not crawl out at once, but makes a little door, or plug, of waste matter and silk, and then rests a while.

The larva grows rapidly, for it has nothing to do but eat and grow. Like all caterpillars, as it grows it sheds its old skin, or molts. Just before a caterpillar molts, it quits eating and seems to be sleepy and tired. It remains quiet for some time, and then the skin bursts along its back. It pushes this backward as it crawls out of the skin, and now it is a larger caterpillar in a bright new "coat."

When full-grown, this caterpillar is less than one inch long and is quite plump and lively. As it moves, one can see its six little front legs, which are its true legs and look like tiny claws. Its eight back legs are fleshy and are called its prolegs, or false legs. At the end of its body is a fleshy prop leg. Its prop leg and prolegs help it hold tight wherever it crawls.

When the codling moth larva is ready, it crawls through the door it made and lets itself down to the ground by a silken thread which it spins as it drops. Then it crawls over to the trunk of the tree and climbs up to hide beneath the bark. There it spins a cocoon in which it changes to a pupa, and then into a little moth as small as a dime. The larvae which spin cocoons in July are ready to fly within a short time, but those which spin cocoons in August remain in them all winter.

The codling moth has delicate antennae and a beautiful brown, mottled body. Its wings are grayish-brown with a bright copper-colored little horseshoe pattern on the front wings and little fringes on the back wings.

Codling Moth

These moths fly to an apple, pear, or quince tree that is blooming and lay their eggs on the young

NATURE READER BOOK 4

fruit as the petals fall. In a few days, the baby caterpillars hatch and begin to burrow into the tiny apple, pear, or quince. That fruit usually does not grow large, for it is **stunted**, or stopped. It falls from the tree early, and the part injured by the larva usually rots. Such fruit does not keep any length of time; and, if packed in a barrel, every apple that touches it becomes rotten, too. The codling moth larvae cause much damage to apple, pear, and quince crops. To prevent this spoilage, fruit trees should be sprayed with insecticide when the petals begin to fall from the blossoms. Then, as the larvae eat into the fruit, they will **ingest**, or take in their bodies, some of the chemical and die.

Winter birds, especially the nuthatches, downy woodpeckers, and chickadees, destroy countless numbers of codling moth pupae during the winter. The chickadees also eat many of the codling moths themselves as they fly about in the spring. If you protect these birds, you will help save the fruit crops.

In some apples a little "worm" without legs may be found. This is the plum **curculio**, or American plum **weevil**, which is also a pest that destroys fruit. One can always tell it apart from the codling moth larva, because the plum curculio is legless. The adult plum weevil has a dark brown body with white and gray patches and large humps on each **elytron**, or wing case. It uses its down-curved mouth to puncture the skin of the young fruit, so it can place an egg in each hole it makes. After the larvae hatch, they eat their ways into the center of the apple, plum, or cherry; then the fruit spoils. The larvae then leave the fruit and bury themselves in the soil, where they change into pupae and eventually emerge as adults.

Review

1. How does the codling moth injure fruit?

2. How can the **orchardist**, one who cultivates an orchard of fruit trees, prevent the codling moth from damaging his fruit?

3. How do our winter birds help save our fruit?

Some Things To Do

Examine a wormy apple carefully to see how the larva ate its way through it. Also watch our winter birds searching the tree trunks for pupae. To protect next year's crop, carefully look at the bark of fruit trees in winter and destroy any pupae of the codling moth.

ABIDE WITH ME

A - bide with me, fast falls the e - ven - tide,

The dark-ness deep - ens, Lord, with me a - bide;

When oth - er help - ers fail, and com - forts flee,

Help of the help - less, O a - bide with me.

Chapter Six
Turtles and Snakes

Turtles

A turtle walks very slowly. It seems to be going somewhere, for it moves steadily; and finally it reaches its goal. If disturbed, it just draws in its head, legs, and tail and feels safe within its shell. Then, if there is no noise, it gradually extends its head, and looks all around to see if the coast is clear. Turtles, as well as snakes, lizards, alligators, and crocodiles are **reptiles**, or cold-blooded animals. A cold-blooded animal is one whose blood is the same temperature as the air about it, while the blood of warm-blooded animals has its own temperature whether the air about it is hot or cold.

The upper shell of a turtle is called the **carapace**, and the lower shell is the **plastron**. In some turtles

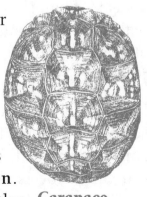

Carapace

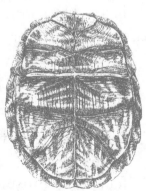

Plastron

NATURE READER BOOK 4

the carapace is arched, while in others it is quite flat. The inner side of the shell is the turtle's ribs; the outside is bony plates covered with beautiful horny shields. The head, legs, and tail are covered with a **scaly** skin and can be drawn completely within the shell by some turtles and partly within by others.

The turtle's head reminds one of a snake's head and is beautifully marked, though differently for each kind of turtle. As the turtle draws in its head, the skin falls into beautiful folds, sometimes forming a pattern or design. Then, when the head is extended, these unfold as the neck stretches. Its pretty little eyes are bright yellow and look intelligent. The turtle has an eyelid that moves upward to cover its eye; this is called a **nictitating lid**—a thin membrane that is drawn across the eyeball for protection. The nostrils are two tiny holes in the snout. The turtle's mouth, or beak, has a sharp, horny edge for biting its food because it has no teeth. Its throat is constantly **pulsating**, or throbbing, as it swallows air for breathing. It also hisses when it is angry.

The turtle's four legs and feet seem to be very soft, but they have bones in them. The back feet have five toes, somewhat webbed, but the front feet have only four. Each toe is armed with a long, slender claw. These help it climb. Once a turtle in a screen cage climbed up the screen sides to the top, a foot and a half from the ground, trying to escape. Another one in a wooden box, the sides of which were quite high, climbed up one side and over the top, and then drew in its head, legs, and tail as it dropped to the floor. There it remained quiet for a while; then it thrust out its head, looked around, extended its legs, and walked away.

A farmer noticed that some creature was feasting on the big ripe tomatoes in the garden, which was at the edge of a cornfield, near a river. One day, a turtle was found clinging to a branch and stalk of a plant while it ate a large red tomato that was

two feet from the ground. It was holding so tight that force had to be used to get it down from the tomato, of which it had eaten more than half.

Turtles eat many insects, vegetables, and berries; and those that live in the water also eat fish and water birds. One day, ducks were heard quacking loudly as they swam on the lake. They were making such a racket that the owner hurried to investigate the cause of the disturbance, and found that a turtle in the water had bitten off a duckling's leg. The wound healed, however, and the duckling grew to be a large, strong duck.

Turtles hatch from eggs. In June or July, the mother turtle scoops out a hole in the soft, damp soil or sand near a stream and deposits from a few to several dozen leathery-skinned eggs. She covers them well with the soil or sand and then goes away and forgets all about them. When the eggs hatch and the baby turtles work their way out of the ground, they actually know which way to go to reach the water and lose no time getting there.

There was a cornfield along a river and, beyond it, a woods where the ground was soft and damp. A big turtle chose this place to make a nest. Late one afternoon, she scooped out a hole and laid her eggs in it. On the ground near her nest were many old leaves which the baby turtles could use as hiding places after they crawl out of their dirt nest.

In the fall, turtles dig themselves into the ground and sleep until spring. This is called hibernating. They never work hard or move quickly, for they are usually safe when drawn within their shell; and they live to be quite old. They make very interesting pets for boys and girls, and some are used for food.

The Wood Turtle

The wood turtle is one of the most common turtles in North America and lives in damp woods and sometimes in the water. Although it can swim very well and hibernates in the water, it is mostly a land turtle. Sometimes it wanders far from its home through woods, meadows, and farmlands. At times, it even tries to cross a road or highway but often does not make it. This rough-shelled turtle is found from Nova Scotia to eastern Minnesota and south into the Virginias.

The wood turtle grows to be about five

Wood Turtle

to eight inches long. Its carapace has many large **scutes**, or horny plates, with **concentric** ridges that rise up like a pyramid. This means that each scute is built of several layers of shell that get smaller until they reach the top, and the outside ridges of these layers have a common center point. At the rear, the carapace is notched and the plastron is deeply notched.

The wood turtle's fleshy parts are reddish orange in color, which gave it its name "redleg" when it was marketed for food in the early 1900s. The wood turtle eats many insects, vegetables, and berries. It is gentle and makes an interesting pet.

The Box Turtle

The box turtle has the front and rear parts of its plastron hinged in such a way that they can be pulled up against the carapace; the shell closes so tight that a knife blade cannot open it. This forms a protective "box" that completely guards its soft parts. This dry-land turtle has a back that is high and arched. The box turtle is only found in North America, from Connecticut to Nebraska, south to the Gulf of Mexico, and into the Southwest and northern Mexico.

This gentle turtle is kept more frequently as a pet than any other turtle. If you keep it as a pet, put

Box Turtle

your box turtle in a fenced area of your backyard or in a box of dirt for it to dig; also add a shallow pan of water for it to drink. It feeds on berries, vegetables, mushrooms, insects, and earthworms. Some people use it for food.

The Painted Turtle

The painted or pond turtle is beautifully colored, having bright red spots on the lower margin of its shell. This smooth-shelled reptile is found in southern California and northern Mexico. It lives in shallow ponds and feeds on plants, insects, fish, water animals, and **carrion**—that is, dead animals. It also likes to bask in the sun on logs or rocks. It makes an interesting pet, too, but is not used much for food.

Painted Turtle

The Snapping Turtle

The snapping turtle lives in sluggish rivers and ponds. It is brownish-gray like the mud in a stream and has broken ridges on its carapace. It is a very vicious fighter. The snapping turtle cannot draw its large head and limbs into its shell; but it has strong, sharp-edged jaws that help to protect it. It eats fish and water animals, and its flesh is good for food, but it does not make a desirable pet because of its mean disposition, or nature.

The alligator snapping turtle is the largest freshwater turtle in North America; it grows over two feet long and normally weighs up to 150 pounds. It has a wormlike part on the bottom of its mouth

Snapping Turtle

that attracts fish as it quietly lies underwater with its mouth open, ready to snap them up.

The Soft-shelled Turtle

The soft-shelled turtle lives in streams. Its round, somewhat flat carapace is covered with a soft, leathery skin that is light olive in color and has no scutes, or plates. Its plastron, however, is light colored and rather small. Its beak is narrow and very pointed; and its neck stretches up and out of the water, allowing it to stay underwater for a long time. This turtle has webbed feet that let it move quickly over land or in water. The soft-shelled turtle is very vicious and fights to escape if caught. It destroys fish that are caught in nets or on lines and also kills water birds. It is largely used for food.

Soft-shelled Turtle

Sea Turtles

The turtles that live in the tropical seas have powerful **flippers** instead of feet with claws. They swim by moving their front flippers up and down, instead of back-and-forth like other turtles. They visit the southern shores of the United States to deposit their eggs. The green turtle is said to have the finest flavor of all the sea turtles and is largely used for food. It eats vegetables and grows so large that it may weigh as much as 700 pounds. Between April and June the female turtle

Green Turtle

leaves the water to lay her eggs during the night. She digs a hole about fourteen inches deep in the sand, where she will lay as many as 200 eggs. Two weeks later she returns to lay more eggs near her first nest. This is called the second crawl.

People can go out very early in the morning, follow the turtle's tracks in the sand, and dig around where the turtle stopped until they locate the eggs. They dig them out with sticks and sell them, because many people like to eat turtles' eggs.

Where men do not rob the nests, the baby turtles dig their way out of the sand and immediately hurry toward the sea. They never make the mistake of going in the wrong direction even if you turn them around. On their way to the sea, they are apt to be gobbled up by pelicans or other water birds, and even those that reach the water are preyed upon by creatures there.

The hawksbill is the most beautiful sea turtle and is found in the Gulf of Mexico and as far south as Brazil. The natives drop an iron hoop, with a net like the crown of a hat, over the sleeping turtle. It becomes entangled in the net and then can easily be brought to the surface. This turtle is valued for its horny brown and yellow layer on the outer surface of its carapace, called a **tortoiseshell**. It is used to make combs and jewelry.

Hawksbill Turtle

Review

1. Give the life history of a turtle.
2. How do turtles escape their enemies?
3. Of what use are turtles?

Some Things To Do

Catch a very small turtle, and make it comfortable in
an aquarium with water in which to swim, and a rock
on which to climb out of the water. Feed it insects,
ant eggs, earthworms, and lettuce. Watch it swim,
walk, rest, and eat. Study its habits.

Snakes

If you are a good observer, you probably can
spot a snake whenever you take a walk in the
woods or through the fields. Perhaps you have
stopped to watch one as it moved gracefully and
swiftly over the rough ground and glided easily
over sloping rocks and through matted grass
and briars.

Snakes are reptiles. They mostly live in the tropics,
but many kinds live in the United States, Canada,
and even as far north as Iceland. They are found in
forests, desert places, grassy lands, swamps, and in
ponds and streams. Some spend most of their
lives on the ground or in the
ground, while others
live in the water.
Some are born
alive, while
others hatch

from white, leathery-skinned eggs that are laid on the ground, or in brush piles, and are hatched by the sun. Some are poisonous, but most of them are not. A poisonous snake can be recognized by its head, which looks like a triangle; and, on its head, the snake has two pits, or holes, between the nostrils and the eyes. The harmless snakes do not have these two pits, and most of them do not have heads shaped like triangles.

Snakes have no eyelids and cannot wink, but their eyes are protected by smooth, clear scales; you can easily recognize these eye protectors if you examine old skins shed by snakes. As snakes grow, they molt. Before they shed their skins, though, the snakes remain slow and quiet for some time; then the skins split at the head, and the snakes wriggle out, sometimes leaving their moist old skins with every scale perfect, including their clear eye scales. Snakes have no outer ears, yet it has been proven that they can sense sounds in the ground and through other solids; but most, if not all, snakes cannot hear sounds sent through the air.

A snake's mouth is very unusual; it can be opened very wide, for the lower jaw is not joined directly to the upper one. In fact, a snake can swallow its prey whole, though it is larger in diameter than

NATURE READER BOOK 4

the snake itself. Its sharp, conelike teeth point backward and are not used for biting or chewing; they are only used for holding prey and forcing it down the snake's throat. Its long, slender, forked tongue can be darted out with great speed, like lightning, and then withdrawn into a covering. A snake that is not poisonous is called **nonpoisonous**, and it swallows its prey alive. People have been known to rescue toads, frogs, and other creatures that have been swallowed by a snake. A snake may even rob the nests in a poultry house, swallowing the eggs whole.

A poisonous snake has **fangs**, besides its other teeth. A fang is a long, pointed tooth which the snake uses to poison its enemies when it bites them. The fangs are not fastened tightly to the jawbone, so that when the mouth is closed, they lie flat against the roof of its mouth, pointing backward. When the snake opens its mouth to strike, some poison is pressed from the glands, or sacs, in the top of its mouth; at once, the fangs drop straight down to their resting position. The two fangs are hollow

Head of a Rattlesnake

with a needle-point opening; through them, the poison oozes into the **incisions**, or cuts, made when the reptile strikes. Sometimes the prey struggles and twists out the loosely attached fangs, but that does not bother or hinder the snake in any way, for there are some new fangs near the base of the ones being used. These fangs will begin to get larger and will soon be ready to take the place of the ones that were lost.

Although snakes have no legs to help them run, they can travel quickly on land and swim rapidly in water of any depth. A snake's backbone is unusually **flexible** and strong and has a pair of long, curved ribs fastened to each **vertebra**—that is, any bone or segment of the backbone. The muscles attached to the ribs help the snake to bend in every possible position. The scales along its back and sides are small, but those along the **ventral**, or belly, side of its body are very broad and overlap like the shingles on a house, with the loose ends pointing backward. These scales are called scutes. As they are waved backward by the muscles, they push the body forward in much the same way as the treads push an army tank along. When swimming, a snake usually holds its head above the water and moves very rapidly.

During the winter, snakes hibernate; but at the first sign of spring, they become active again and leave their winter shelter, whether it was a stone pile, a hollow beneath a stone, or a hole in the ground. Before summer, the eggs are laid; or, in the case of some species, the young are born alive.

Snakes do much good in destroying harmful rodents, such as gophers, rabbits, squirrels, rats, and mice, as well as harmful insects; they should not be killed even though they do eat some toads, frogs, and birds that are beneficial. Many people are afraid of snakes and kill every one they see; but if they observed one closely, they would find it most interesting and might overcome their fear. Parts of North America would be overrun with rats, mice, and gophers if it were not for snakes, owls, and hawks. The owls and hawks can get these rodents when they are in flight, but snakes can follow them into their burrows and kill them. Most snakes are absolutely harmless to man and should be protected so that they can destroy these pests. Hawks, **roadrunners**, king snakes, and people destroy many snakes.

The Rattlesnake

There are about thirty species of rattlesnakes, or pit vipers, in the Western Hemisphere; all of them are poisonous, and all have the "rattle" at the end of the tail. Each time the snake sheds its skin, a little cap of skin is left at the end of its tail, so that after several molts, the snake has a rattle. If everything is favorable, the snake will shed three times a year, getting a new rattle with every "coat." The old skin splits along the head, and the snake crawls out, dressed in a bright new skin, larger than before. If it is a dry year, the rattlesnake may shed its skin only twice, getting two new rattles instead of three. Then, too, the oldest rattles—being on the very end of the tail—are frequently broken off when the snake crawls over rough places. If its tail is tapering and still has the "button" on the end, you can estimate the snake's age by counting three rattles for every year.

Rattlers also have a pit between each nostril and eye. When hunting, they use these pits to help them sense the body heat of their prey. They are yellowish-brown with cross bands of bright-brown edged with black and fringed with yellow.

Rattlesnake

141

Rattlesnakes are very poisonous but do not "spit" poison—though you may see some dripping from the tips of their fangs as the snakes spring forward. Their poison is harmless on unbroken skin; it is dangerous only when it enters the blood stream. Before striking, these snakes shake the tips of their tails, causing their rattles to make a sound like the rattling of dried seeds in pods. Rattlesnakes coil themselves tightly, getting enough **leverage** on the ground, and then throw half of their bodies forward as they strike their prey. Thankfully, they will not attack a person unless disturbed.

Rattlesnakes can swim, though they do not like the water. They eat rats, mice, and other rodents, feeding about three times a week; but they themselves often fall prey to the roadrunner, hawk, and king snake. Their young are not hatched from eggs but are born alive.

The eastern diamondback rattler inhabits sandy places in the southern part of the United States. It is the largest rattlesnake in the world, often attaining a length of eight or nine feet; and it has fangs one inch long. The common timber, or banded, rattler inhabits woody and rocky places in the Mississippi Valley, while the Pacific rattler is found in the western part of the United States.

The Copperhead

Copperhead Snake

The copperhead, another poisonous snake, is found near water in woody, rocky parts of the central and eastern United States. This member of the viper family is also called a highland moccasin. The poison from this snake is not very strong and is rarely fatal to humans. Its color is a pinkish brown, like two shades of copper—old and new; and its back is crossed with dark spots resembling dumbbells, making it blend so well with clumps of dead grass and fallen leaves that one can hardly see it. Like the rattlesnake, the copperhead also has two pits between the nostrils and the eyes, but it does not give any warning before it strikes its prey. It likes to eat rodents and other reptiles. Its young are also born alive.

The Water Moccasin

The water moccasin, or cottonmouth moccasin, is another poisonous snake with two pits between the nostrils and eyes. This member of the viper family inhabits streams of the southeastern United

States, where it preys on fish, frogs, and small animals. It does not bother man unless disturbed or cornered. Many persons call every water snake a water moccasin, but the real water moccasin is brown with black or gray spots on its abdomen, its scales are like beads, and it has the two pits between the nostrils and eyes. Common water snakes, however, have no pits, have reddish spots on the ventral—or belly—side, and are not

Water Moccasin

poisonous. The cottonmouth gets its name because, when it opens its mouth, one can see the puffy, white **membrane** that lines it. The young of the cottonmouth are born alive and manage to get along by themselves.

The Coral Snake

True coral snakes belong to the cobra family and are confined to the tropical areas of the Western Hemisphere; but there are similar snakes in Africa and Asia. The largest of the coral snakes is very poisonous and lives from the southern United States—especially in Florida—all the way to northern Argentina. Coral snakes require a very warm temperature, hide much of the time, and are very ferocious when feeding. Their fangs are very short, but their **venom** is more deadly than that of the rattlesnake. Even so, coral snakes are easy to handle and rarely bite if people pick them up, yet their venom can kill a man. Most of the more than fifty species have broad black and red rings, separated by narrow yellow rings. Since their colorings warn us that they are poisonous, it is helpful to remember the following rhyme:

> Red touches yellow,
> Dangerous fellow!

There are false coral snakes that look like true coral snakes, because they also have red, black, and yellow rings—but their red rings do NOT touch their yellow rings. These harmless snakes belong to the colubrid family—a group

Coral Snake

of nonpoisonous snakes. In South America, they live in the forests. They have fangs in the rear of their mouths. False coral snakes of North America include the scarlet snake and the scarlet king snake. The scarlet snake is a small, nocturnal snake that likes to burrow in the ground. It is found in the United States from New Jersey to Florida and as far west as Texas. The scarlet king snake is a small species that lives in the southeastern part of the United States. It is called a "king" because it eats other snakes, even poisonous ones! It kills by **constricting**, or squeezing, its prey to death. It also eats small mammals, **amphibians**, birds, and birds' eggs.

The Water Snake

The water snake lives in damp, marshy places, near streams or ponds, and is often seen sunning itself on the shore, or resting on a branch of a tree

Blotched Water Snake

that overhangs the water, where it can slip into the water and escape at the least sign of danger. It has an unusually stout body with ridged scales. It is brown with dark brown spots, and is light on the ventral side. If cornered, it will get ready to attack and give off a very disagreeable **musk**, or odor, from glands at the base of its tail. The young are born alive and learn to live on their own, feeding largely on minnows. Water snakes eat frogs, salamanders, fish, and crayfish, which they pursue in or near the water; and they, in turn, may be gobbled up by a bass.

The King Snake

The king snake is a harmless, nonpoisonous snake that belongs to the colubrid family. It has a long, slim body that is black or brown with different patterns; and it can move very rapidly.

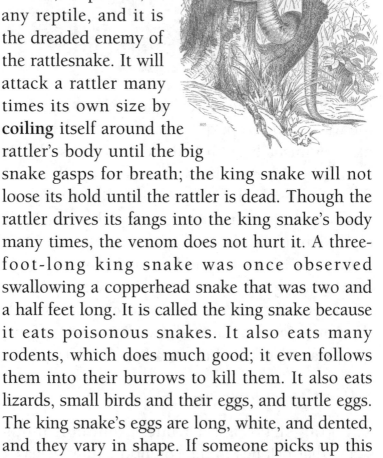

Mole Snake

(type of King Snake)

Its scales are smooth, while those of a rattlesnake are ridged. A king snake is **immune** to the venom, or poison, of any reptile, and it is the dreaded enemy of the rattlesnake. It will attack a rattler many times its own size by **coiling** itself around the rattler's body until the big snake gasps for breath; the king snake will not loose its hold until the rattler is dead. Though the rattler drives its fangs into the king snake's body many times, the venom does not hurt it. A three-foot-long king snake was once observed swallowing a copperhead snake that was two and a half feet long. It is called the king snake because it eats poisonous snakes. It also eats many rodents, which does much good; it even follows them into their burrows to kill them. It also eats lizards, small birds and their eggs, and turtle eggs. The king snake's eggs are long, white, and dented, and they vary in shape. If someone picks up this snake, it will give off a very disagreeable odor, but it is **docile**, or easy to handle. Toward rodents and snakes, however, it is bold and fearless.

The Milk Snake

The milk snake is a brightly marked member of the king snake group. It eats other snakes, rats, mice, and insects; it even pursues rats and mice into their burrows to crush and kill them. It lives near, or in, barns and dairies where it can find rodents. It does not steal milk from cows as some people believe, for it does not touch milk that is given to it in captivity; but it is especially fond of rats and mice. When approached, the milk snake vibrates its tail, hisses, and then strikes. If handled by people, it is not as docile as other kinds of king snakes and may bite without warning. It is gray, with brown or chestnut saddlelike marks, bordered with black. Its eggs have a soft, leathery skin and hatch in about seven weeks.

The Garter Snake

The garter snake is another harmless snake that gives off musk which has an unpleasant, sweet odor. It gets its name from the fancy garters that men used to wear to hold up their socks. It is found throughout much of North America, from southern Canada to Costa Rica. It usually has a light-colored stripe down the center of its rounded back, with black and yellow, or beige, stripes on either side; some even have blue stripes. It is an excellent swimmer. It feeds on frogs, toads, salamanders, fish, tadpoles, and earthworms; sometimes it eats small mammals, birds, and carrion. A large bass, however, will eat a garter snake and relish it. Most garter snakes are docile, but some may strike without warning. The young are born alive and learn to live on their own.

The Ribbon Snake

The ribbon snake is a striped, harmless snake that also gives off musk when threatened. It is the most slender and brilliantly-colored member of the garter snake group, and its habits are consistent with other garter snakes. The ribbon snake is found among the tall hedges and **vegetation** around pools and ponds. It swims at the surface of the water instead of diving like a water snake. The ribbon snake protects itself by threading its way through the underbrush and escaping from sight with amazing speed. It likes to eat frogs, salamanders, and small fish like other garter snakes, but it will not eat earthworms.

Ribbon Snake

The Blacksnake

The blacksnake, or northern black racer, lives in dry, rocky regions, and is satiny black with a white throat and chin. This member of the colubrid family is found from southern Maine to central Alabama. It is slender and can move with great speed. It does not fight unless cornered and is not poisonous, though it may tear one's skin with its teeth. It swallows its prey whole. A blacksnake was once observed in a tree, robbing a blue jay's nest and swallowing one of the young birds. It destroys many rats, mice, and other rodents but will also get into a henhouse and swallow the eggs.

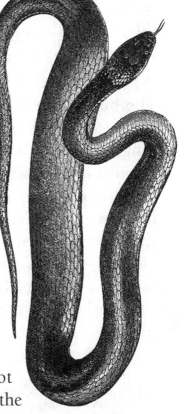

The blacksnake's eggs have a tough, white, leathery skin and are laid under rubbish. The young ones hatch in about two months and take care of themselves.

The black rat snake, or pilot black snake, is also found in the

Black Racer

eastern United States and usually grows to be about four feet long—but may grow more than eight feet long! This member of the colubrid family lives in woodlands or around farm buildings. It hunts rats and mice and constricts, or squeezes, them until they die. The black rat snake also likes to eat eggs; some are called chicken snakes because they like to raid henhouses. This snake is black, with a whitish chin and throat, like the black racer; but it has slightly keeled, or turned up, scales on the upper side of its body.

The Bull Snake

The bull snake is the largest of the harmless North American snakes, growing up to six feet long; it gets its name because it hisses loudly when it is approached or annoyed. It may bite, but it is not poisonous. Other members of the bull snake group are the gopher snake—found in the southwestern United States and northern Mexico—and the pine snake— found east of the Great Plains. The bull snake is yellow, with black

Bull Snake

or chestnut-colored marks, and is very gentle. It is at home on the plains and likes to hide in clumps of vegetation or burrows where mammals used to live. The bull snake also has an enlarged nose plate which makes it a good burrower. It does much good destroying rats, mice, rabbits, and squirrels. Like the king snake, the bull snake kills its prey by coiling itself around it, or by constriction. It is especially fond of birds' eggs.

The Hognose Snake

The hognose snake, sometimes called the "spread-head" or "puff adder," is another one of our harmless snakes and

Hognose Snake

is a splendid bluffer. If disturbed, it will hiss loudly, spread its head to nearly twice its natural width, and even pretend to have a spell of convulsions; finally, it will roll over on its back and **feign**, or pretend, death. One of these snakes was teased until it hissed, then it was caught behind the head and held prisoner for a moment or two. When it was laid on the ground again, it pretended to have a convulsion and vomited a plump three-inch frog that it had swallowed whole a short time before. Then it turned over on its back and lay as if it were dead.

This snake has a short, broad head that is large. Its upturned snout gives it its name. Its body is stout with a very short tail and it grows to be about two or more feet long. It is usually brown, with dark, square marks on its back, and its belly is light and mottled with gray or green. It lives near springs and creeks where it feeds on toads and sometimes frogs.

The Green Snake

The green snakes are slender, graceful, and grassy-green in color. They are found in North America, parts of Africa, and eastern and southern Asia. As commonly found, the smooth-green snake has sleek scales and feeds almost entirely on insects and spiders. This gentle "green grass snake" has a plain bright green back and a plain white, or pale yellow, belly. It lives mostly on the ground and is found in the north central and northeastern parts of the United States, the Rocky Mountains, and southeastern Texas.

Green Snake

The rough-green snake is found farther south, from the Ohio River basin to the Gulf of Mexico, and from the Atlantic Ocean to the Great Plains. Its keeled, or ridged, scales help it climb vines in search of insects to eat; this is why it is sometimes called the vine snake. Its eggs are white, leathery, and long and are laid under stones. The green snake makes a very interesting pet.

The Glass Snake

The glass snake—often called the horn snake or joint snake—is not a snake at all; it is a legless lizard. How is this lizard different from a snake? First, it has movable eyelids and external ear openings, which a snake does not have. It also feels stiff compared to a snake. In addition, its tail is very long—sometimes two or three times the length of its head and body combined—compared to a snake's tail.

Like other lizards, it sometimes sheds its tail when in danger and then grows a new one that will be somewhat shorter. Often, when it breaks off, the tail will divide into many pieces, as glass would do if it fell on something hard, and so it gets the name of

Glass Snake

glass snake. It is a harmless creature that lives in loose soil among leaves and grass, or under roots or stones. The glass snake feeds on insects, spiders, snails, birds' eggs, and small snakes and lizards. It has scales that are strengthened with bony plates. This makes the glass snake stiff, but God gave it deep, flexible grooves that run along each side of its body. These grooves allow it to expand when it eats or when the female has eggs.

The Hair Snake

The hair snake is not a snake either, but a worm that lives in the water. Many people formerly thought that it came from a horsehair placed in the water. This hairworm, or horsehair worm, lays its eggs in the water, and then the tiny young burrow into the foot of some water insect—or some other **arthropod**—and work their way into its body. This insect, in turn, is swallowed by a fish, in whose intestinal tract the worm changes; after five or six months, this creature emerges into the water as a hair worm. Some adult hair snakes grow to be over three feet long— that is, a meter (about 39 inches).

Hair Snake

Review

1. How can you recognize a poisonous snake?
2. How can snakes swallow their prey whole?
3. How do they use their teeth?
4. Where are the fangs and how are they used?
5. How can snakes travel so fast though they have no legs?
6. How do snakes grow?
7. Of what use are snakes?
8. Why should harmless snakes be protected?
9. Give one interesting fact about each of the following snakes: rattlesnake, copperhead, water moccasin, coral snake, water snake, king snake, milk snake, garter snake, ribbon snake, blacksnake, bull snake, hognose snake, green snake, glass snake, and hair snake.

Some Things To Do

With a parent or qualified nature guide, try to observe how a live snake travels. Notice how its movements affect the grass or weeds through which it glides. Remember that many snakes are poisonous, so be very careful when doing this activity.

The Doxology

Praise God from whom all blessings flow,
Praise Him all creatures here below,
Praise Him above, ye heavenly host,
Praise Father, Son, and Holy Ghost.

Rev. Thomas Ken

Chapter Seven
The Toad, the Bat, and the Beaver

The Toad

Have you ever watched a toad hop? Did you see how he blinks his eyes? He looked so contented, as if nothing bothered him.

A toad is not always able to hop. The first part of its life is spent in the water. In May or June, the mother toad lays 600 to 30,000 eggs—depending on the species—in some pond or quiet water along a stream. They are in long tubes of a jellylike substance and are deposited on the bottom of ponds or attached to water plants. The

eggs are round, like tiny black pills. Later they become longer; and, finally, little **tadpoles** emerge and wriggle in the jellylike substance which protects them. In a few days they usually manage to get out and swim away.

At first the little tadpole has no mouth. A little bump, where the mouth would be, helps it hold tight to a water plant while it rests head upward. When it is about three days old, little tassels can be seen on both sides of its throat. These are the gills by which it breathes. The blood, passing through these gills, is purified by coming in contact with the air in the water. About ten days later, a membrane grows down over the gills and covers them so that they are on the inside of the throat instead of the outside. If you look carefully, you can see a little opening, or breathing **pore**, in the left side of the tadpole. The water is taken into its mouth through its nostrils, flows through an opening in its throat, passes over the gills, and goes out through this little opening.

The tadpole's little round mouth is constantly opening and shutting as it searches for food. It feeds on the slime in ponds and can bite off pieces of plants with its horny jaws. As the tadpole grows older, its mouth gets larger and wider, like a toad's mouth, and its eyes begin to bulge, like those of a toad.

Its long, flat tail is used in swimming. It pushes the water, first on this side and then that, sending its body in any direction. Some people say that a tadpole eats its tail or bites it off. What really happens is that its growing body **absorbs**, or takes in, its tail. You can even see it gradually shrivel or get shorter as the legs develop.

Another unusual thing happens to the tadpole. When it is a month or two old, you can see a pair of little back legs growing. These have webbed feet with five toes and are used in swimming. About two weeks later, a pair of little front legs, or arms, begins to show, the left one growing out through the breathing pore. These front legs have little feet, or "hands," that are not webbed and are used for balancing. As its tail shrivels, the tadpole uses its back legs for pushing and its front legs for balancing in the water. If the tadpole happens to lose a leg, another one will grow in its place. The tadpole often comes to the surface to get more air for its gills, until, on a rainy day in July, it swims to the shore, steps out of the water, and walks away on the ground, toeing in as it goes. It has become a toad and can breathe air.

The toad has a brownish-colored back and a lighter-colored belly. On its back are many warts, or poison glands, in which there is a substance that is very disagreeable to most animals that try to devour the toad. However, snakes, hawks, owls, and crows do not seem to mind the poisonous fluid, for they eat many toads. The toad's skin is very dry and feels cold when one touches it, because the toad is a cold-blooded animal. A cold-blooded animal is one whose blood is the same temperature as the air about it, while the blood of warm-blooded animals has its own temperature whether the air about it is hot or cold.

Surinam Toad
(with young escaping
from cells on mother's back)

The eyes of the toad bulge and are very beautiful, for they shine like gold. Watch it wink by pulling its eye down into its head. An eyelid moves upward from below—an eyelid which moves upward in this manner is called a nictitating lid. When sleeping, the toad's eyes are drawn in, and do not bulge. Its tiny nostrils are black. Its ears are little, flat, oval spots behind its eyes and a little lower down. Its mouth is wide, and its jaws are horny. The toad has no teeth and swallows its food whole. It can not breathe as we do, for it has no ribs by which to inflate its chest; instead, the toad has to swallow the air and force it into the lungs. That is why its throat is constantly pulsating, or throbbing.

The toad's long, strong back legs help it jump. It will jump up two feet to catch its prey, and will take long leaps to escape an enemy. When it is greatly frightened, the toad flattens itself out on the ground, and looks so much like a clod of earth that it often escapes the keen eyes of an enemy. Sometimes it pretends to be dead if it is seized, but when it is about to be eaten, it sends out heartrending cries.

The toad hops and walks. It is very sensitive to heat and hides under leaves, rubbish, stones, or plants during the day, coming out about twilight to search for bugs and insects. Often the toad digs itself in; that is, it kicks up enough earth with its back legs to make a little hole into which it fits, completely covered with soil and hidden. If it rains hard during the day, toads will come out of hiding to enjoy hopping about in the water. They appear so suddenly that many persons think it actually "rains" toads.

A toad sheds its skin several times a year. It seeks a sheltered place where it remains quiet for some time. Then its old skin splits and peels off or is removed by its "hands," and the skin is then eaten by the toad. Its new skin is brighter than the old one, and, of course, each time the toad sheds its old skin, it is larger.

The toad moves very slowly as it stalks its prey. Suddenly it thrusts out its tongue, which is attached to the lower jaw at the front of its mouth, touches the insect, and holds it fast, for there is a sticky substance covering its tongue.

Quick as a flash the prey is swallowed. A toad in a cage ate enough insects in one day to fill its stomach four times. Most of the bugs that toads eat are harmful to the farmers' crops. It has been estimated that one toad eats more than nine thousand harmful insects in three months.

It is amusing to watch a toad eat an earthworm. The toad walks around the worm to seize it by the head, evidently knowing that the worm's horny hooks extend backward and will rasp its throat if swallowed the wrong way. If the worm is too large, the toad uses its "hands" to stuff the worm down its throat. When swallowing a large mouthful, the toad closes its eyes, giving the impression that it is thoroughly enjoying the meal. It never drinks water with its mouth but absorbs the water through its skin; the toad likes to stretch itself out in shallow water until its thirst is quenched. It must have moisture or it will die.

In winter, a toad burrows deep into the ground and sleeps until the warmth of spring awakens it. This is called hibernating. Once a gardener working late in the fall dug up a big, plump toad. Its legs were flat against its body, its eyes were not bulging, and it did not move a muscle but seemed to be dead. The gardener put the toad back into the hole, hoping that it would not be harmed by the experience. The following spring, a toad that looked just like the one the gardener dug up was found in the garden.

The toad's song is a **crooning** sound, like a trill way down in its throat. When singing, its throat is puffed out like a ball. In the spring, the toads come out of the ground, and the mother toads return to the pond in which they lived as little tadpoles to lay their eggs. Then you can hear them singing.

Toads do so much good that people should not harm them; they destroy **cutworms**, beetles, weevils, caterpillars, grasshoppers, crickets, spiders, earthworms, centipedes, millipedes, ants, and other creatures, including **snails** and **slugs**. Yet many are killed when mowing the lawn or burning off a field; boys who are thoughtlessly cruel also kill many toads. Some people keep toads in their cellars to rid them of insect pests, because toads eat roaches as well as other insects. In the city, one can see toads beneath the street lights, eating bugs that fall to the ground after hitting the light. Watch a toad when you see one, but do not harm it.

Review

1. Give the life history of the toad.

2. Why should toads be protected?

Some Things To Do

Visit a pond to get some toad eggs and some water for an aquarium. Watch the eggs hatch. Feed the tadpoles and watch them develop into toads. Set them free in your garden to destroy insect pests for you.

The Bat

Have you ever watched bats flying around at dusk and wondered why they dodge so much? The bat is a very interesting and useful little animal that looks like a mouse but can fly like a bird. Some people call them "flitter mice."

A common type is the little brown bat whose body is the size of a little mouse and whose fur is short and silky. It has a playful little face, with small eyes that are set deep in its head, a little pug nose, and a little pink mouth that opens wide, showing very tiny, sharp teeth. Its little ears stand erect. The little brown bat weighs a fraction of an ounce and is only three inches long, including its inch and a half tail.

Its wings are wonderful. They are joined to the sides of its body and are very long, often nine inches from tip to tip. They are a delicate, thin, rubbery skin, which is called a membrane. This membrane is not only stretched over a bony framework that is like very long fingers, but extends back to the bat's ankles and then to the tip of its tail. Three of these "finger bones" extend out into the wing like the ribs of an umbrella. There is a useful little hook where

Skeleton of a Bat

they are joined. The bat uses its wing hooks to drag itself along the ground, to climb, to hold onto the bark when resting, to help support itself when asleep, and to scratch its little head.

The bat's tiny feet have five very slender toes with sharp hooked claws by which it can hang all day when it is sleeping. That part of the membrane between its ankles and tail can be folded like a pocket to catch insects as it flies.

The bat is a remarkable flier. It can turn sharply, dodge in and out, up and down without stopping or ever bumping into anything—not even a twig. Its sense of hearing is very keen, and it can tell by the rebound of sound when it is near an object.

Both sides of the wing membrane are covered with very fine hairs that are connected in some way with delicate nerves, so that the bat knows when one of its wings is near anything, and it dodges. It can fly very swiftly through trees and not touch a twig.

The bat likes to wash itself. One was kept in a cage for a while and studied. The little creature licked its wing, washed its head and face with the front part of its wing, and then licked it again. It

licked its foot and
rubbed it over its head
and then licked it again.
It was fun to watch the
bat stretch its wings
like rubber when it
washed them. It lost no
time in climbing up the
sides of its screen cage
using its feet and two
wing hooks. It lapped up
the water from the person's

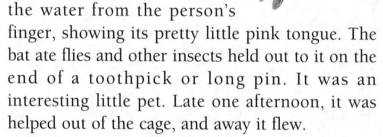

**Fruit
Bat**

finger, showing its pretty little pink tongue. The
bat ate flies and other insects held out to it on the
end of a toothpick or long pin. It was an
interesting little pet. Late one afternoon, it was
helped out of the cage, and away it flew.

Sometimes bats are seen resting head downward
among the tree tops during the day. From below,
they look like brown withered leaves. If one is
touched, though, away it flies in a hurry to find
another resting place. Bats do not chatter like
squirrels; they squeak when they communicate
with each other. If frightened, their squeaks are
different from those given when all is well.

Bats do not lay eggs like birds, even though they
do have wings and fly. In summer the mother bat
has one tiny baby, which she nurses and cradles

in the folds of her wings. Until her baby is too heavy for her, she carries it clinging to her neck when she flies about catching insects. When her baby grows larger, she hangs it on a twig before she flies after bugs, and returns at short intervals to feed it.

Bats do so much good by destroying mosquitoes, codling moths, and other insect pests, that we should never harm them. If a bat happens to get into your house, open the doors and windows so it can fly out again. It was an accident that it entered, for bats do not like to be in people's homes; and they do not harm people, though many people are afraid of them.

In winter, bats hide in eaves of buildings, hollows of trees, or some protected place where they sleep until spring. Some bats migrate southward in the fall and return in the spring. In warm countries, there are several kinds of bats, some of them quite large.

Review

1. How does a bat differ from a bird?

2. How does it resemble a mouse?

3. Why should we protect bats?

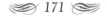

Some Things To Do

Watch bats as they hunt insects. Notice how close they fly to twigs without ever touching them. Look closely at trees to see if you can discover a bat resting, head downward, among the leaves. If you discover one resting within reach, your dad could wear heavy gloves, catch it, and put it into a wire cage; then you could keep it for a day or two. Feed it insects on the end of a straw, toothpick, or piece of wire. Observe how it eats. Sprinkle water in a part of the cage and see how it drinks. Observe how it climbs and hangs.

The Beaver

One of the most remarkable of the wild animals found in North America is the beaver. It is a skilled lumberman, an engineer, and a builder.

The beaver is at home in the water because it is an aquatic animal. It is also a nocturnal animal, coming out of its home at night or late in the afternoon. In North America, it is the largest of the gnawing animals, or rodents—some others being rabbits, **porcupines**, squirrels, rats, and mice. The beaver's color varies, being sometimes reddish-brown, sometimes grayish-brown, and often dark brown. The beaver has two "coats" of fur. The undercoat is soft, silky, short, and thick;

the outercoat is made of long, coarse hair that sheds water like a raincoat.

A beaver is much plumper and rounder than a dog, and its legs are shorter, too. It sometimes weighs as much as sixty or seventy pounds. Its total length is about forty-two inches, including its tail, which is about sixteen inches long. Its skull is massive and very strong, and its head is short and round, with a blunt nose, small, deep-set eyes, and short round ears. A beaver has four very sharp, strong, chisel-like front teeth that are yellow or orange in color and are self-sharpening. These are the beaver's **incisors**, which are used for cutting. There is quite a space between them and the **molars**, which are the teeth used for chewing and are far back in its mouth.

The beaver cannot see very well but has a very keen sense of smell and hearing.

The beaver's strong, scaly tail is long—about half the length of its head and body—broad, and flat, and is shaped like the paddle part of an oar. When standing on its back legs to work, the beaver braces itself with its tail, and when swimming, it uses its tail for a rudder; but it never uses its tail like a trowel to pat or plaster mud. It signals with its tail by whacking it down hard upon the water, making a noise like a giant firecracker.

Its four strong legs are so short that the beaver is very awkward on land. It has five toes on each foot—the powerful back feet being webbed. The front feet, which are a little smaller, are used skillfully like hands to push branches, pieces of logs, and other material through the water. The beaver can carry mud between its front feet and its chin while it swims with its back feet. The claws on the beaver's toes are very strong and the second toe on each back foot has two claws instead of one. One of these claws is regular and the other extends sidewise. People who have observed the beaver carefully are undecided as to how the animal uses these double claws, but a beaver was once seen using them for a toothpick to remove a splinter from between its teeth. Just as a dog will scratch its ear with its back foot, so a beaver could easily use this double claw on its back foot to remove a splinter of wood that had lodged between its teeth.

Before cutting down a tree, the beaver walks slowly around it, looking upward as though studying its growth. Then he sits up on his back feet, bracing himself with his tail as a pet dog would do if you told it to sit up. The beaver rests his forepaws against the tree, and then works very much as a lumberman would. First, he bites out a chip above, and then one below, with his strong incisors; then he drives his long, powerful teeth behind the part left between the two cuts, and pries or pulls out the chip. This he does all around the tree, until it begins to quiver and is about to fall. Then the beaver sounds a warning by whacking his tail upon the ground, and hurries to his pond where he will be safe from any enemy that happens to investigate when the tree falls.

Sometimes one beaver acts as a sentinel to warn the others at work on trees, if they are a little distance from the water. Some beavers were once at work, each gnawing an aspen tree about four inches in diameter. Another beaver was some distance away and out of sight of the workers. Suddenly this one got the scent of wolves and signaled it to the workers by leaping up on his back legs and standing for several seconds. Then it ran to the pond. At the same moment, the beavers working on the trees made a dash for the pond, too. There was so much noise from a neighboring waterfall that the beaver could not have been heard if he had whacked with his tail, as they usually do in signaling; that is why he signaled the scent by standing up. In a few minutes, two wolves appeared where the beavers had been at work.

The beaver seems to forget all about a tree he **fells**, and cuts down another some distance away from it. There may be ten or fifteen trees lying on the ground where they fell when he cut them. Later, the beavers come back and cut the branches off the trees. Then the logs are cut into lengths of three to six feet or more, dragged or rolled to the water, and floated to the food pile near the house. Here they are sunk to the bottom of the water and held by mud and other logs piled on top. Beavers prefer to use trees less than eight inches thick but they have been known to fell trees as large as thirty inches in diameter.

When a pair of beavers decide to build a home, they first select a suitable site where they can easily get food. They prefer a valley that is somewhat narrow, through which a small stream with a sluggish current flows. After thoroughly exploring the stream above this point to make sure that they will not be endangered by sudden floods, the beavers construct a dam that may be straight or irregular, and probably is narrow. At points where they expect floods, they make a much broader dam, and shape it like a crescent, curved toward the current. This kind of a dam is strengthened by the pressure of the water. The beavers may also construct a second dam several hundred feet below the first one, so that the water

between the two serves to support the first dam, and is easily held in check by the second one. Sometimes the base of the dam is several yards wide, slanting to a much narrower top in order to ease the flow of water during a flood.

The beavers use mud, reinforced by sticks that are two to several inches thick and three feet or more in length. They push or guide the sticks through the water with their forepaws and swim with their back feet and tail. The beavers carry the mud in their forepaws against their chins and pile it on the sticks and twigs. They pile rocks on the sticks to hold them in place. All sorts of floating material lodge against the dam and help to strengthen it.

The beavers seem to know soils, for they use watertight clays in their construction work, and these become almost as hard as reinforced concrete in keeping out the water. Much of the wood they use in making the dam is green and will begin to grow after a time, adding strength to the structure. Seeds will be brought by the water, too, so that one will see grass, brush, and trees growing on the dam. Often the beavers scoop up mud from the bed of the stream with their back feet, making a ditch or moat in front of the dam. This loosened mud is carried by the water and lodges between and against the sticks in the dam.

The dam causes the water above it to spread out and become a wide pond. In this the beavers construct their house of mud, sticks, and rocks. They begin on the floor of the pond and build the bottom of the house from twelve to twenty feet across, shaping it like a cone, rounded at the top, so that it rises from three to six feet above the surface of the water. It looks just like a pile of mud, sticks, and rubbish in the water, but it is really a clever piece of work. There is a large room inside, just above the water level so that it is always dry.

The walls of this room are about a foot thick and very hard and strong, so that when the pond is frozen in winter and the beavers' fierce enemies can cross the ice to reach the house, they cannot dig through the walls to get their prey. If the weather is very cold, one can see vapors rising from the house, showing that the beaver has some system of **ventilation**. Two or more tunnels lead into the house from beneath the water, so that the beavers can swim about even if the pond is frozen.

If conditions are such that the beavers cannot construct a dam to form a pond in which to build their house, they will tunnel some distance into a steep bank along a stream so that their room at the end of the tunnel will be above the flood stage of the river. The entrance to their

tunnel is under the water. Although these are called bank beavers, they are no different from the house beavers. A pair of beavers may leave their house to travel, and not finding a suitable new place in September, will live in the bank of a stream that winter. The next winter they may again live in a house.

Beavers also have their winter supply of food stored on the bottom of the pond. They eat the bark of aspen, poplar, alder, willow, and birch; and, in summer, they feed on berries, roots of water lilies, and grasses. If a cornfield is near, they will also eat some corn or, if an orchard is near, the bark of fruit trees. They place a pile of short logs and branches of their favorite food trees on the bottom of their pond, holding them in place with mud. In winter the beavers can easily carry some of these into their house and when they have eaten the bark, they again place them on the bottom of the pond to be used for repair work on the dam, if necessary.

Beavers are sociable animals; that is, they like company and get along very well with their friends and neighbors. If many of their favorite food trees grow near a stream, several families will make homes there. Each family builds its own house, but all help with the dam and the food supply. Sometimes the beavers cover their group of houses with a dome that may be fifteen feet wide at the surface of the water and rise above the water eight or ten feet. We call this a colony house. Each family's house, then, is really an apartment in the colony house.

From two to eight—usually four—**kits** are born in a beaver family during the latter part of May or early in June. The parents take them on an outing in August, sometimes traveling miles from their

home to other beaver colonies. Beavers travel during late summer, and if they happen to be at another house when the weather becomes cold, they will lay in their food supply and remain there for the winter. Beavers mate for life, and as they grow older, they do not travel, but live in the same home year after year. During the summer, many beavers gather on sand bars and sandy beaches to rest, play games, and have a general good time. They thoroughly enjoy a sun bath in the sand, but at the least sign of danger the beavers plunge into the water and are gone. It is then that they live on the roots of water plants and the bark of shrubs along the shore.

When the beavers have to fell trees some distance from their pond in order to store their winter supply of food, they dig a canal to the group of trees and then tow the wood down to the pond. This canal may be a few feet or several hundred feet long, from one to three feet deep, and two or more feet wide. Beavers even dig canals in the bottom of shallow ponds to make it easier to travel in winter when the water is frozen. They can swim a long distance under water.

If the dam springs a leak, the beavers immediately detect it and get busy. Without showing themselves, they look over the situation; they find where the hole is and decide how to repair it quickly. They get wood from the pile of sticks from which the bark has been eaten, carry it to the break, and force it in place. Beavers have been observed forcing a two-inch stick downward as a stake is driven, using teeth and claws to do it. If the break is very large, they may even cut a **submerged** tree, working under the water for as long as eleven minutes at a time. Then the cut tree is towed to the break and let float, bottom end first, over the dam, so that it will come to rest on the bottom of the stream with its top leaning against the dam. Then the top is cut off even with the surface of the water, the smaller branches used like stakes, and the chinks filled in with mud. Beavers are both industrious and cautious workers.

Beavers are so interesting and so much valued for their beautiful fur, that many of our states have passed laws protecting them. In colonial days, they were so common and their fur so valuable, that their pelts were used instead of money among the Indians, white trappers, and traders. In Alaska, beaver pelts were the medium of exchange until the discovery of gold there. In the latter part of the eighteenth century, American companies exported 150,000 skins annually, and the Hudson Bay Company 50,000 more.

The long, coarse hairs are pulled out of the fur, leaving the beautiful soft, silky, thick undercoat, which is very valuable and is still used for ladies' coats. Many Indians that live in northern and central Canada and Alaska eat beaver meat and like it; these Indians also use beaver fur for clothing and blankets. Bears, wolves, **wolverines**, mountain lions, and other wild animals prey upon beavers.

Review

1. Describe a beaver.
2. How does it fell a tree?
3. Give reasons why we call the beaver an engineer.
4. How does it prepare for winter?
5. How does the beaver show intelligence? Patience? Industry?

Some Things To Do

Construct a model of a beaver colony house. Show the beavers at work as lumbermen and engineers.

Words You Should Know

A

Abdomen—that part of an insect's body behind the thorax

Absorb—take in or assimilate

Alight—land or come to rest, as a bird on a perch

Amphibian—a cold-blooded creature that lives the early part of its life in the water (aquatic) using gills and then on land after developing lungs

Apiary—place in which a colony of bees is kept; Apiary comes from the Latin word *apiarium* which means "beehive."

Aquatic—living in the water

Arbor—a latticework shelter covered with vines

Arthropod—creature with an exoskeleton (no backbone), segmented body, and jointed limbs; arthropods include insects, arachnids (spiders, etc.), crustaceans (crabs, shrimp, wood lice, etc.) and myriapods (centipedes and millipedes).

B

Bantam—very small chicken; *–adj.* tiny, feisty

Bars—bands or stripes of color on a bird; also barred

Beebread—a mixture of pollen and nectar fed to the grubs of bees

Brood— *n.* a number of young (chicks) hatched at one time; –*v.* incubate, sit upon (eggs) to hatch

Brush—shrubs and small trees growing wild

Burrow—a hole in the ground made by an animal for shelter

C

Camouflage—protective disguise

Carapace—the upper shell of a turtle

Carrion—dead animal; rotting flesh

Cicada—a large insect with a stout body, wide, blunt head, and large transparent wings; often called a locust

Coax—persuade or urge gently

Coiling—winding

Colony—group of creatures that live together

Compound eye—a large eye that is made up of many little eyes and looks like honeycomb under a magnifying glass

Compound Eye

Concentric—having the same center, like circles within circles

Constricting—drawing together or crushing; squeezing

Coot—a small, sooty-colored wading bird that resembles a duck; its bill is narrow; its toes have lobes instead of webs; its cry is very harsh.

Covey—a flock of wild fowls, such as quails

Crane fly—a very long-legged, slender insect that resembles a giant mosquito

Crayfish—a freshwater crustacean which looks like a small lobster; also called a crawfish or crawdad

Crest—topknot; tuft of feathers on a bird's head

Crooning—humming or singing in a low tone

Curculio—a beetle that injures fruit

Crayfish

Cutworm—a caterpillar that hides in the soil during the day and cuts off young plants at night

---

D

Disposition—unique attitude of a person or thing

Diurnal—moving about or seeking food during the day and sleeping at night

Docile—easy to handle; readily trained

Down—soft feathers that certain baby birds grow; under plumage of geese and ducks

Drone—male bee

E

Elastic—can be stretched like rubber

Elytrons—wing cases (or forewings) of insects, such as beetles, used to protect the back wings

Excavate—dig out or make (a hole) by removing dirt or soil; to scoop out

---

F

Fangs—long, hollow teeth of poisonous snakes

Feign—pretend or put on the appearance of

Fell—cut down; to cause to fall

Ferocious—wildly harsh; extremely brutal or cruel

Flash colors—colors that can only be seen when the bird spreads its tail or flies; usually white and found somewhere on the tail.

Flexible—easily bent

Flippers—broad, flat limbs used for swimming, as those of a seal

Foliage—the leaves of trees and plants

Foundation—prepared base or ground on which some building or structure is built

Fringed—edged; "fringed with down" means "feathers edged, or tipped, with down"

G

Gills—the breathing organs of aquatic animals

Gourd—hard-shelled fruit of a gourd plant

Grubs—the larvae of beetles and bees

H

Hibernate—sleep or exist in a dormant condition all winter

Hollow—hole; shallow valley

Honeydew—the sweet substance given off by aphids and other small insects

Hooting—calling of an owl

Hover—move the wings up and down so as to remain in one place in the air

Aphid

I

Imbedded—laid deep in a substance

Immune—exempt or free from

Incision—a cut

Incisors—teeth used in cutting

Indigestible—cannot be digested or converted, as into a form of food that can be used by the body

Indigo bunting—small, canarylike bird that is indigo blue

Ingest—take (a liquid or food) into the body

Insecticide—chemical used to kill insects

Iridescent—having colors like the rainbow

J–K

Jimson weed—a poisonous plant that belongs to the nightshade family; has foul-smelling leaves, prickly fruit, and trumpet-shaped flowers that are white or purple in color; named after Jamestown, Virginia, which was shortened to jimson

Kit—a young fox, beaver, cat, or other small furbearing animal; kitten

---

L

Leverage—the power or force obtained by pushing against something

Lumber—move clumsily or heavily, as in flight

M

Malaria—disease carried by mosquitoes; causes chills, fever, and sweating that keep returning

Mandibles—upper and lower parts of a bird's bill

Mealybug—scalelike insect covered with a white powdery wax that it discharges; feeds on plants

Membrane—a delicate, thin, soft, rubbery skin

Metallic—like metal

Metamorphosis—remarkable change in form that an insect goes through during its life, from one stage to another—egg, larva, pupa, and adult

Midrib—the main rib of a leaf

Migrate—to travel from one area or climate to another, as certain animals do every year

Molars—the teeth used for chewing

Mole—a small animal with short, silky fur, that burrows in the ground

Molts—sheds its "coat" of skin or feathers

Moonflower—climbing vine that grows rampantly and has six-inch white, fragrant, night-blooming flowers and contains a milky juice used for gelling Castilla rubber; one of the largest of the morning glory family

Mottled—marked with spots of different colors

Mouser—animal that catches mice

Musk—very disagreeable odor given off by an animal or plant for protection

Mythology—made-up stories about pagan gods and goddesses who supposedly lived long ago

---

N

Native—person, animal, or plant that is born in or belongs to a certain place or region

Nectar—the sweet liquid in a flower

Nesting site—the place where a bird builds its nest

Nestling—a very young bird

Nictitating lid—thin membrane that is drawn across the eyeball for protection; *nictitating* comes from the Latin word that means "to wink."

Nocturnal—moving about or seeking food at night and sleeping during the day

Nonpoisonous—not poisonous; harmless

Nymph—larva of certain insects that undergo incomplete metamorphosis

---

O

Orchardist—one who cultivates an orchard or plantation of fruit trees

Oval-shaped—shaped like an egg

Owlet—a young owl

P

Paralyze—make helpless, so (victum) cannot move

Parasite—a plant or animal that clings to and feeds upon another living plant or animal

Pellet—ball of indigestible parts (bones, fur, etc.) that an owl vomits after eating; mud ball of wasp

Plantain—small plant that has a dense tuft of basal leaves and a long, leafless stalk with a spike of small flowers on top

Plastron—the lower part of a turtle's shell

Plumage—feathery covering of a bird

Porcupine—a large, clumsy, slow-moving rodent that has stiff spines or quills mingled with its coarse hair; climbs trees to cut the tender bark

Pores—very tiny holes

Poultry—domestic birds used for their meat and eggs, such as chickens, turkeys, ducks, and geese

Praying mantis—strong greyish-brown or green insect about two or three inches long; holds up its two stout front legs ready to seize and eat any insect that comes near it

Preen—dress or smooth (feathers) with the beak or bill

Probe—search or examine carefully

Prolegs—extra sets of "legs" which are attached to the abdomens of caterpillars and other larvae; these prolegs are different from their true legs, which are attached to their thoraxes.

Protrude—thrust forward

Pulp—a soft mass of animal or vegetable matter

Pulsating—beating or throbbing

Pupil—the opening of the eye through which light passes

R

Radiate—spread outward from a center point in all directions, like rays—as with feathers around an owl's eye

Rail—secretive bird with short wings, narrow body, and long toes; lives mostly in marshes

Radiating Feathers around Eye of Owl

Reel—unwind silk from a cocoon

Reptile—a cold-blooded animal that crawls or creeps

Roadrunner—a peculiar bird of the southwestern United States; runs down the road very swiftly, often traveling faster than a horse can trot

Robber fly—fly that resembles a bumblebee and preys on other insects

Rodents—animals that gnaw

Rosettes—bunches that look like tiny rosebuds

Rudder—vertical blade at the end of a boat or plane, used for turning it through the water or air

---

S

Salvia—any of the various *Salvia* plants belonging to the mint family that have opposite leaves and whorled flowers

Scale insect—small plant-sucking insect; female is often covered with a waxy discharge that resembles scales

Scaly—covered with scales

Scutes—wide scales on the belly of a snake or shell of a turtle

Scale Insect and Scales

Segments—the parts of an insect's body that look like rings

Sentinel—guard or sentry; person or thing that stands watch

Silo—a tall, round structure for storing fodder, or green food, for cattle, horses, etc.

Slugs—soft creatures that look like snails without their shells

Snail—a soft creature with a spiral shell on its back into which it can easily crawl

Sociable—living in one large company or group

Species—a class, or group, of creatures that are alike in several ways; distinct sort or kind

Sphinx—refers to an ancient, imaginary Egyptian creature that had the body of a lion and the head of a man, or some other animal; there is a large stone Sphinx near the pyramids in Giza, Egypt. A sphinx usually brings to mind the idea of a scary monster in ancient literature.

Sphinx

Spindle-shaped—round in the middle and tapering toward each end

Spiracle—a breathing hole in the side of an insect

Stunted—stopped or arrested, as the growth of a creature or plant

Submerged—sunk in water

Suet—hard, fatty tissue from farm animals

Superstitious—marked by foolish fear of what is unknown or mysterious

T

Tadpole—the early stage of a frog or toad

Talons—the claws of a bird of prey

Tapers—gets smaller toward one end

Tawny—a dull, yellowish-brown

Thorax—that part of an insect to which the legs and wings are attached

Tortoiseshell—the shell of the hawksbill turtle

Towhee—bird about the size of a robin; black above, with a white breast and reddish-brown sides; also called the "chewink"

Tremulous—quivering

Tubercles—little knobs or bumps on insects

Tufts—small bunches of hair or feathers growing together

V

Vegetation—trees and plants growing

Venom—poison

Ventilation—supplying with fresh air

Ventral—the underside

Vertebra—one of the bony parts of the backbone

Vibration—the rapid back and forth, or up and down, movement of wings, etc.

Vital—belonging or essential to life

Voracious—greedy in eating

W

Warble—sing or whistle with trills or vibrating tones, as a bird

Weasels—small, slender-bodied animals that have short, brownish fur and feed on other animals

Weevil—a small beetle whose larva destroys much grain

Weevil

Whetted—sharpened

Whirring—buzzing or whizzing

Wireworms—larvae of certain beetles; feed on the roots of plants

Wolverine—strong, stocky, furbearing animal of the weasel family; very ferocious and is found in the Northern Hemisphere

Y

Yellow fever—disease carried by mosquitoes; causes fevers and often death; ruins the liver